BOOK 4

New Horizons in ENGLISH

LARS MELLGREN
MICHAEL WALKER

Consulting Editor: JOHN A. UPSHUR
English Language Institute
University of Michigan

 ADDISON-WESLEY
PUBLISHING COMPANY
Reading, Massachusetts
Menlo Park, California • *Amsterdam*
Don Mills, Ontario • *London* • *Manila* • *Singapore* • *Sydney* • *Tokyo*

Taped Material, Book 4

Six cassettes in a vinyl album
Running speed: 3 ¾ ips
Running time: approximately four hours

Reel to reel tapes available upon request

Illustrations by Akihito Shirakawa

Photographs: p.7, courtesy of Ford Motor Company;
p. 121, courtesy of New England Dragway.

TO STUDENTS AND TEACHERS

In our opinion, the object of every English class for speakers of other languages should be the use of the language in everyday situations. That's why we try to build up a useful vocabulary within a certain number of grammar patterns.

The language should be used—and used in a meaningful way. Students should learn to express their opinions and feelings, to give and receive information, to say what they mean.

It is essential that students take a very active part in the learning. We think they should work together often in pairs, or in bigger groups. They should also feel that they are making constant progress in their studies. Accordingly, the first tasks in each unit are easy, but grow harder as the book continues. Throughout the book, students can test themselves and experience the pleasure of personal growth and progress.

We hope you will find the *New Horizons in English* series an effective and entertaining way to learn and use the English language.

Lars Mellgren
Michael Walker

CONTENTS

In this unit we are going to read and talk about cars and drivers.

We are going to study and practice making sentences with words like these:

safe, safer, safest
economical, more economical, most economical
good, better, best

We are also going to use these vocabulary words:

acting	lighter (*adj.*)	ships
amazed	maximum	short cut
around	mechanical	station wagon
back seat driver	mileage	successful
brakes	mines	sum
citizens	motor	suppose
during	nervous	tank
economical	pedestrian	vehicle
farthest	powerful	wages
fast	price	wood
fond	producing	workers
founded	safe	worse
gasoline	salesman	worst
leather	scooter	

—Slow down! You're driving too fast.
—I'm only doing fifty.
—But the speed limit's thirty here.
—Don't worry. There aren't any police around.
—Watch out for that pedestrian!
—Hey, who's driving? Me or you?
—You are. But. . .
—Stop acting like a back seat driver.

STUDY AND PRACTICE

Mr. Mendes has gone to a car dealer's to look at a new car. He asks the salesman all about the latest station wagon. He is very fond of his old car, but the salesman tries his best to sell him a newer one.

—Is it good?

—But is it fast?

—Is it safe?

—Is it economical?

—Is it easy to drive?

—And is it comfortable?

—I suppose it's expensive . . .

—Well, my old car is the cheapest one I've ever owned. I'll keep it.

—Yes, it's the best one we have.

—Yes, it's the fastest one we have.

—Yes, it's the safest one we have.

—Yes, it's the most economical one we have.

—Yes, it's the easiest one we have.

—Yes, it's the most comfortable one we have.

—Yes, it's the most expensive one we have.

—John's **sports car** is very **fast**.
—Is it as **fast** as Bill's?
—Oh, yes. It's even **faster**.
—Really? I thought Bill's was the **fastest** one made.

| 1. limousine | expensive | more expensive | most expensive |

| 2. sedan | economical | more economical | most economical |

| 3. motorcycle | powerful | more powerful | most powerful |

| 4. scooter | safe | safer | safest |

| 5. station wagon | good | better | best |

| 6. old car | bad | worse | worst |

Practice making sentences with the words below.

A	taxi bus limousine	takes	more less fewer	passengers gas luggage	than a ....

A	scooter sports car sedan	doesn't take	as much as many	gas passengers luggage	as a ....

—Don't **stop** here.
—Why not?
—That sign says **"No Stopping."**

1. **park**   **No Parking**

2. **turn**   **No Left Turn**

3. **walk**   **Don't Walk**

4. **pass**   **No Passing**

5. **enter**   **One Way**

READ AND UNDERSTAND

Henry Ford

One day in 1893 the citizens of Detroit, Michigan were amazed to see a motor vehicle coming down the street. The driver's name was Henry Ford.

Henry had been interested in mechanical things even as a young boy. His mother had died in 1875 when he was only twelve. At school he was not a good student. His father wanted him to become a farmer, but Henry's dream was to make cars.

In 1903 he founded the Ford Motor Company. His idea was to make cars that were lighter, cheaper, and faster. His most successful car was the Model T. Ford sold fifteen million between 1908 and 1925. By 1924 the factory was producing 7,500 cars each day. Ford's cars were cheap because he had his own factories for most things he needed—glass, leather, wood. He had his own mines. He even built his own ships and planes.

Ford paid his workers high wages. All of them got at least five dollars a day, which was a large sum in those days.

1. Why were the people of Detroit amazed?
2. What do you know about Ford's parents?
3. What were Ford's plans for cars?
4. In what way was the Model T successful?
5. How was it possible for Ford to make cheaper cars?

The end of the line at a Ford factory in 1913.

By 1922, ten million Fords had been produced. Ford had his picture taken between two famous models–the very first, and the ten millionth car he had made.

DIALOGUE

How do you like my new car?

It's much bigger than your old one.
It's much faster than your old one.

Are you nervous?

Yes, you're driving too fast.

Don't worry. I've got good brakes.
I never worry about the speed limit.

Why did you turn here?
Is this the right way?

I always take this short cut.

But that sign said | No Left Turn. Do not Enter.

That's just during rush hour.
Is that why all the traffic is going the other way?

I wish you'd slow down.

Would you rather walk?

I don't mean to be a back seat driver.
Keep your eyes on the road!

Well, you're acting like one.
I am, but you're making me nervous.

I've had enough. Stop the car.
You're nervous? Stop the car.

I can't.

Why not?

Can't you read? That sign says No Stopping!

MIXED BAG

1. 1973 Mercedes-Benz
    Price: $ 7,500
    Maximum speed: 80-85 miles per hour
    0 to 60 miles per hour: 18 seconds
    gasoline mileage: 35 miles per gallon

2. 1973 Jaguar
    Price: $ 9,300
    Maximum speed: 135 miles per hour
    0 to 60 miles per hour: 7.2 seconds
    gasoline mileage: 13 miles per gallon

3. 1973 Volkswagen
    Price: $ 2,299
    Maximum speed: 81 miles per hour
    0 to 60 miles per hour: 21 seconds
    gasoline mileage: 25.5 miles per gallon

1. Which is the most expensive car?
2. Which is the cheapest car?
3. Which is the fastest car?
4. Which is the slowest car?
5. Which car travels farthest on one tank of gas?
6. Which car travels the shortest distance on one tank of gas?
7. Which of the three cars would you rather own? Why?

UNIT TWO
Preview

In this unit we are going to read and talk about science fiction.

We are going to study and practice making sentences with words like these:

marvelous — marvelously	never	often
quiet — quietly	hardly ever	seldom
happy — happily	sometimes	once a . . .
	frequently	every . . .
	always	now and then

We are also going to use these vocabulary words:

anxiously	driveway	magnificent	ray (*gun*)
attacked	elegant	marvelous	robot
behave	explosion	must	saucers
breathe	fooled	mysterious	scream
brightly	flash	neither	shining
broadcast	frequently	normal	soldiers
calmly	germ	now and then	sounds *(n.)*
careful	grandparents	object *(n.)*	stood
careless	harmless	opposite	such
continued	heard	planet	superb
correct	holes	pointing	useless
creature	impatient	polite	weapons
customs	invaders	poll	war
	invention	proud	

WARM-UP

—You say you saw a creature from another world?
—Right! He had four arms and three eyes!
—You're kidding.
—No, I'm not. He acted very strangely.
—I don't believe you.

—Hello. I'm taking a poll for a radio station.
  Do you believe in flying saucers?
—No, I don't.

READ AND UNDERSTAND

Invaders from Mars

In 1938 a play called "The War of the Worlds" was broadcast on the radio. The play started with a news flash about a mysterious explosion on the planet Mars. Then there was a report about a burning object falling over a farm in New Jersey.

At the same time the play began, America's most popular radio show was ending on another station. Many listeners missed the very beginning of "The War of the Worlds." When they changed stations, they did not know that it was just a play. They thought what they were hearing was really happening.

As the play continued, a reporter described the strange object. He said it was shining brightly and hard to look at. Suddenly a door opened. There was a scream, and the reporter was dead. Six thousand soldiers attacked the object, but only 120 lived to tell about it.

Of the six million or so people who heard the play, more than two million thought it was a true news report. People anxiously telephoned the radio station for news. Thousands left their homes to escape the Martian invaders. It was many days before life was back to normal.

How did the play end? Neither the Army, the Air Force, nor the Navy could stop the Martians. All their weapons were useless. Finally, the invaders were killed by a little germ. It was harmless to people from earth, but deadly to the Martians.

1. How did the play start?
2. Why did many people miss the beginning?
3. How did the reporter describe the object?
4. What happened to the soldiers who attacked the object?
5. How were the Martians finally stopped?

STUDY AND PRACTICE

The Professor and his Robot

Professor Player is very proud of his latest invention, a robot. He loves to tell people how good his robot is. A reporter from the Daily News is interviewing the professor.

—I've never heard of such a robot. Is he good at everything?

—Oh, yes. He does everything well.

—They say he's a marvelous tennis player.

—That's right. He plays tennis marvelously.

—And that he is a magnificent singer.

—True. He sings magnificently.

—And a wonderful painter.

—Correct. He paints wonderfully.

—I even heard that he was an elegant dancer.

—Yes, he dances elegantly.

—I suppose he must be a very quick learner.

—Of course. He learns very quickly.

—They say he is a superb chess player.

—That's right. He plays superbly.

—But how come your robot is so good at everything?

—Well, he has such a wonderful father, you know!

He was **quiet**.	He answered **quietly**.

1. impatient
2. pleasant
3. sad

4. clever
5. careless
6. polite

He answered **angrily**.	He was **angry**.

1. happily
2. calmly
3. politely

4. correctly
5. sadly
6. carelessly

The boys were **happy**. They played **happily**.	They smiled **happily**. They were **happy**.

1. The teacher was impatient.   He spoke. . .
2. The girl ran quickly.   She was very . . .
3. I spoke patiently.   I was . . .
4. She is a careless pupil.   She answers . . .
5. The man shouted angrily.   He was . . .
6. Marie is very polite.   She always speaks . . .
7. "Yes," she said happily.   She was very . . .
8. She's an elegant dancer.   She dances . . .
9. He sang magnificently.   He was . . .
10. She gave a quiet answer.   She answered . . .

1. —My brother is always very **careful.**
   —How does he drive?
   —He drives . . . .

2. —My brother is always **polite.**
   —How does he speak?
   —He speaks . . . .

3. —My brother is always **nervous.**
   —How does he behave?
   —He . . . .

4. —My brother is always **patient.**
   —How does he teach?
   —..............

5. —My brother is always very **quick.**
   —How does he work?
   —..............

I'm not like my brother at all. I'm just the opposite!

1. How do I drive?   You drive . . .
2. How do I speak?
3. How do I behave?
4. How do I teach?
5. How do I work?

Use the words in the boxes to talk with a friend about things you both do.

Do you	go to the movies play tennis travel visit your grandparents go shopping go swimming speak English	once a year? once a day? every day? now and then? every week?

Yes, I No, I	never hardly ever sometimes frequently always often seldom	. . . .

Now ask a friend if:
1. he (she) travels frequently.
2. he (she) goes to the movies now and then.
3. he (she) goes shopping every week.
4. he (she) plays golf.
5. he (she) often visits the library.
6. he (she) always studies hard.
7. he (she) plays the piano every day.
8. he (she) exercises now and then.

DO YOU TRAVEL FREQUENTLY?

DIALOGUE

News Room.

I'd like to report a flying saucer!
A spaceship just landed in my yard!

Where did you see it?
Not in the flowers, I hope.

You must take me seriously!
It's right in my driveway!

You're kidding, of course.
You must be joking.

I've never been more serious!
Please listen carefully!

What's happening now?

The door is slowly opening!
It's moving slowly towards me!

Is anybody coming out?
Can't you tell it to go away?

There's a big ray gun on it!
A thing with four arms!

Don't shout.
Try to talk calmly.

The gun is pointing at me!
Each arm has two hands!

I'm beginning to believe you.
Come on. A joke's a joke.

You must believe me!
He's got me! I can't breathe!

I'll call the police.
You must be crazy.

Arghhhhhhhhhhhhhhhh!
Ha! I fooled you!

MIXED BAG

Suppose some Martians really landed on Earth. What would they think of Earthmen and their customs? They would probably think we were very strange. When they had returned to Mars, they would tell their friends about some of the things they had seen on Earth. Can you guess from their descriptions what the Earthmen were doing?

1. They took some grass or weeds and rolled it in a piece of paper. Then they pushed it in a hole in the top of their body and set fire to it! What a lot of smoke!!

   ....

2. They sat down in front of a box. At first there was nothing. Then there was a lot of light, and sounds came out of the box. None of the Earthmen moved. I thought they were dead. But then the light and sound stopped and they all got up again.

   ....

3. She put her finger in some holes in a black object. In her other hand, she held something next to her ear. Then she talked to herself for a few minutes! What a strange way to behave!

   ....

4. I saw what must be a game they play. A lot of Earth people stood outside a building. A bell rang and they all went in. Later a bell rang again and they all came out. A few minutes later the bell rang again and they went back in! They did this all day.

   ....

UNIT THREE
Preview

In this unit we are going to read and talk about different kinds of entertainers and entertainment.

We are going to study and practice making sentences with **what** and **what a.** We are going to work with many descriptive words.

We are also going to use these vocabulary words:

actor	entertainment	perfect
actress	enthusiastic	performance
ad	exactly	performer
appearing	excellent	purse
audience	familiar	real
autographs	fantastic	resist
beer	fascinating	reviews
brilliant	freezing	seasick
business	gasped	shocked
charity	idol	simply
check (*n.*)	insisted	sounds *(v.)*
climate	in person	speech
club	jealous	stage
conductor	live (*adj.*)	star
critics	marched	stranger
definitely	musician	teen-age
directions	orchestra	whether
dressing room	ours	yours
entertainer	pale	

WARM-UP

—Did you see the Bobbie Bix Show on TV last night?
—Yes, I did. He's my idol!
—He's a great singer, but it wasn't a live show.
—You mean the performance was recorded?
—Yes, he was appearing at the Apollo Theater last night.
—I think he sounds better on stage.
—Yes, but he's not as handsome in person.

READ AND UNDERSTAND

The Teen-age Idol

Show business isn't as wonderful as it may look. I remember the time my girl friend and I went to see Taggy Montag. We saw an ad in the newspaper for a show he was doing in town. I called the club and got two seats at a table next to the stage. What luck, I thought then. Taggy had been a favorite of ours for a long time. He didn't smoke or drink. He had grown tired of the life of a teen-age idol. He lived simply, and gave most of his money to charity.

The show was a great success. What a fantastic performer the man was! The audience became more and more enthusiastic after every song. After the show, Taggy signed autographs backstage. We were first, since we were sitting next to the stage. Then we couldn't find our way out through the big crowd. Suddenly, we found ourselves outside Taggy's dressing room. We couldn't resist a look inside. Then we heard somebody coming. I don't know why, but we hid in the closet. Out in the dressing room, we heard Taggy and a musician friend talking. "Give me some beer, " said Taggy. "And write out a check for charity. Let the press take a few photos of it and then burn it. I don't work just to give my money away."

I looked at my girl friend. She had turned red with anger. We opened the closet door, threw our autographs on the table, and marched out of the room. Taggy Montag must have spent one or two unhappy hours wondering whether we would go to the newspapers with the "real" Taggy Montag story . . . but we never did.

STUDY AND PRACTICE

—She's a **great actress.**
—Yes, and what a great **film** this is.

---

1. **superb writer**   novel
2. **brilliant performer**   performance
3. **wonderful singer**   song
4. **fantastic entertainer** show
5. **marvelous guitarist**   concert

—He writes wonderful songs.
—Yes, what wonderful songs he writes.

---

1. He produces fine records.
2. He makes successful films.
3. She tells fascinating stories.
4. They give terrible concerts.
5. They sing awful songs.

> —Isn't this **fine music?**
> —Yes, what **fine music.**

1. **marvelous acting**
2. **awful entertainment**
3. **bad luck**
4. **sad news**
5. **expensive furniture**
6. **terrible singing**

Complete these sentences with **what** *or* **what a.**

1. .... good movie.
2. .... good acting.
3. .... terrible actors.
4. .... wonderful entertainment.
5. .... wonderful entertainer.
6. .... wonderful shows.
7. .... fine concert.
8. .... marvelous singing.
9. .... fine singer.

—What kind of **actor** is he?
—A **terrible** one.
—How does he **act?**
—**Terribly,** of course!

1.	conductor	brilliant	conduct	brillantly
2.	painter	wonderful	paint	wonderfully
3.	dancer	superb	dance	superbly
4.	singer	pleasant	sing	pleasantly
5.	writer	poor	write	poorly

—Do you like my new **dress?**
—It's **wonderful.**
—Do you really think so?
—Yes. You look **wonderful** in it.

1. terrific

2. marvelous

3. elegant

4. great

—What do you think of this **record?**
—It's **marvelous.**
—I'm glad you like it.
—It sounds really **marvelous.**

1.	orchestra	fantastic	2.	song	beautiful
3.	speech	brilliant	4.	music	wonderful

> —How did you know he was **ill?**
> —He turned **pale.**

1. seasick   green
2. angry   red
3. jealous   green
4. shocked   white
5. freezing   blue

> —What happened **when he saw the police?**
> —He became **nervous.**

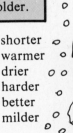

1. while he waited   impatient
2. when he heard the news   worried
3. when he read the report angry
4. when he lived alone   bored
5. when he paid the bill   upset

> —It's cold this winter.
> —Yes, the winters are getting colder.

1. It's dark early these days.   shorter
2. It's warm this summer.   warmer
3. It's dry this month.   drier
4. This lesson is hard.   harder
5. The weather is good.   better
6. The climate is mild.   milder

DIALOGUE

Did you see Bobby Bix on TV?
Have you seen Tom Turnings's latest movie?

No, I'm afraid I missed it.
I never watch TV.

Well, you really missed a great program.
He's never been better.

I know the critics just loved it.
It got very bad reviews.

I like to make up my own mind.
I never read what they say.

So do I.
Neither do I.

He's better on stage than he

is | on TV.
     in the movies.

Yes, definitely.
I wouldn't say that.

Live performances are always better.
Live performances can never be perfect.

Yes, but they make mistakes.
But they're more exciting.

What are you doing tonight?

I'm going to | the theater.
                watch TV.
                the movies.

Can I come along?
Come over and watch it here.

Sorry. I'm going with Susan.
I'm going to watch it at Susan's.

MIXED BAG

Meeting A Star

On Saturday morning at 9:30 I was walking down High Street looking for a record shop. A man stopped me and asked me the way to the Ritz Hotel. I wasn't sure exactly where it was, but I walked with the stranger to the end of High Street. He was very friendly and likeable. I was sure that I knew him—his face looked so familiar. Then I remembered where the Ritz was and gave him directions. He thanked me and tried to give me something. I thought it was money, and said 'no' at first. He insisted, however, so I took it.

I went back to the record shop and listened to a few records. The "Fantastic Five" had a new record that was number two in the top twenty. I decided to buy it. I looked in my purse for my wallet and found the piece of paper the stranger had given to me. It was a photo. I gasped! No wonder his face had seemed so familiar. It was the singer in the "Fantastic Five!"

Now you try to write a story like this. Here are some questions to help you if you find it difficult, but try to write your own story.

1. Where were you?
2. What were you doing?
3. What was the time?
4. Who stopped you?
5. What did he/she want?
6. What was he/she like?
7. Did you know him/her?
8. Where did he/she want to go?
9. How did you help him/her?
10. Did he/she give you anything?
11. How did you discover who the stranger was?

UNIT FOUR
Preview

In this unit we are going to read and talk about social customs and manners.

We are going to study and practice making sentences with:

myself	my-mine
yourself	your-yours
himself	his-his
herself	her-hers
yourselves	our-ours
themselves	their-theirs

We are also going to use these vocabulary words:

acceptable	fault	mine
allow	hers	nobleman
amused	immensely	peas
behavior	impolite	possibly
chance	knife	remember
coincidence	lap	served
considered	manage	social
differ	manners	theirs
especially	matter	uncomfortable
	mention	
	might	

—After you.
—No, after you.
—Oh, I'm sorry.
—Excuse me. It was my fault.

—Could you possibly . . .?
—Of course.
—That's very nice of you.

—Not at all. Hey! That's my . . .
—But you said . . .
—I didn't mean . . .
—Oh, sorry.

READ AND UNDERSTAND

Social Customs and Behavior

Social customs and ways of behaving change. Things which were considered impolite many years ago are now acceptable. Just a few years ago, it was considered impolite behavior for a man to smoke on the street. No man who thought of himself as being a gentleman would make a fool of himself by smoking when a lady was in the room.

Customs also differ from country to country. Does a man walk on the left or the right of a woman in your country? Or doesn't it matter? What about table manners? Should you use both hands when you are eating? Should you leave one in your lap, or on the table?

The important thing to remember about social customs is not to do anything that might make other people feel uncomfortable—especially if they are your guests. There is an old story about a rich nobleman who had a very formal dinner party. When the food was served, one of the guests started to eat his peas with a knife. The other guests were amused or shocked, but the nobleman calmly picked up his knife and began eating in the same way. It would have been bad manners to make his guest feel foolish or uncomfortable.

1. Where was it once considered impolite to smoke?
2. On which side of a woman does a man in your country walk?
3. What did one of the dinner party guests do?
4. What did the nobleman do?
5. Why did he do that?
6. What are one or two very *impolite* things a person might do in your country?

STUDY AND PRACTICE

—Who made **your breakfast?**
—I made it **myself.**

1. Tom's lunch
2. the girls' dinner
3. Aurora's dress
4. your bookcase
5. their costume

—What's the matter with **you?**
—I just made a fool of **myself!**

1. Mary
2. father
3. those boys
4. Jack
5. you two

—Did **you** have a good time last night?
—Yes, **I** enjoyed **myself** immensely.

1. Jack
2. your sister
3. your guests
4. you and your wife
5. you

> —Isn't this my **book?**
> —No, it isn't. It's **mine.**
> —Are you sure?
> —Yes. **I** bought it **myself.**

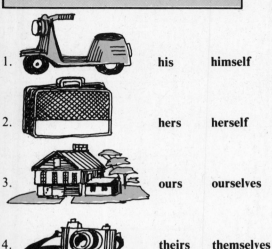

1. his himself

2. hers herself

3. ours ourselves

4. theirs themselves

> —Does that **car** belong to **Tom?**
> —No, it doesn't. It's not **his.**

1. you

2. the Browns

3. your mother

4. Jack and Jane

> —I have a book.
> —Whose book is it?
> —It's mine.

1. Mary has a record.
2. We have a dog.
3. They have a new car.

4. Tom has a tape recorder.
5. I have a watch.
6. The Millers have a new baby.

DIALOGUE

Here, let me do that.
Allow me.

That's very nice of you.
Thank you so much.

Don't mention it.
It's a pleasure.

Haven't we met somewhere
before?
Don't I know you?

Not that I know of.
Do you?

Your face seems familiar.
Weren't you at the Goodson's
party?

Oh, yes. I remember you now.
You were sitting beside me.

Did you like the party?
Oh, yes. I remember you now.

Mmm, I enjoyed myself.
Where do you get off?

This is my stop.
I get off here.

So do I.
This is my stop too.

What a coincidence.

Let me take your bag again.
Here, I'll carry that.

That's okay. I can carry it
myself.
Thanks, but I can manage.

I'm down here to meet a
reporter.

You don't mean Leslie Roberts,
do you?

Yes, how did you know?
Don't tell me you're . . .

That's right.
That's who I am.

Well, how do you do?
Pleased to meet you.

How do you do?
Nice to meet you . . . again!

MIXED BAG

What Do You Say?

1. You meet somebody in the morning.
2. You're introduced to somebody.
3. You step on somebody's foot.
4. You can't hear what somebody is saying.
5. You thank somebody who has just helped you.
6. Somebody thanks you for helping him.
7. You have been to a very nice party, and are leaving now.
8. Somebody has helped you carry some heavy packages.
9. You need somebody to help you push your car.
10. You meet an old friend you haven't seen in a long time.

What's the Word?

1. Sarah acts in the movies; she's an ....
2. Peter is a songwriter; he ....songs.
3. He turned ...., he was so jealous!
4. This lesson is hard, but tomorrow's will be even ....
5. The performance wasn't recorded—it was ....
6. If the book belongs to you, it's ....
7. If the scarf belongs to Mary, it's ....
8. This pen doesn't belong to me—it's not ....
9. Don't I know you? Your face seems so ....
10. We met by chance—it was quite a ....

TEST YOURSELF

I.

(1)   1. I have to stop at a service station before I run out of **g**.................

2. Buses, trucks, and cars are all motor **v**.................

3. My father works in a **f**................. where cars are made.

4. This is their most **e**................. car. It costs $90,000!

(2)   5. You don't have to be frightened. It's quite **h**.................

6. Everyone likes him. He's very **p**.................

7. You cannot take guns or any other **w**................. onto an airplane.

8. I don't like this TV show. See what's being shown on another **s**.................

(3)   9. It's been a very **d**................. summer—it hasn't rained since Spring.

10. I'm very **e**................. about this idea. I really like it.

11. The star talked to the press in his **d**................. **r**.................

12. I've never seen such a **t**................. show. It was really bad.

(4) 13. In most countries it is **i**................. to put your feet on the table.

14. This chair is so **u**................. Have you got a softer chair?

15. —Thank you very much.
> —You're welcome.
> —It's very nice.
> —After you.

16. —Tom, this is Jack.
> —I'm sorry.
> —It was my fault.
> —Pleased to meet you.

17. —This car is terribly noisy.
> —Pardon?
> —Don't mention it.
> —Not at all.

II. *Fill in with* **more, less, fewer, much,** *or* **many.**

(1) 1. There are................. more people here today than yesterday.
  2. A bus takes................. passengers than a taxi.
  3. This car takes................. gas than my old one.

III.

(1) 1. Is your car good? Yes, it's the .... I've ever had.
  2. Is your car economical? Yes, its the ....
   I've ever had.
  3. Is it safe? Yes, it's the .... I've ever had.
(2) 4. That's a good piano.   It sounds ....
  5. She's a good tennis player.   She plays ....
  6. He was angry.   He gave an .... answer.
  7. They answered angrily.   They were ....

IV. *Fill in with* **what** *or* **what a.**

(3) 1. .... wonderful film.
  2. .... wonderful actors.
  3. .... wonderful acting.

V. *Fill in with* **you, yours, yourself,** *or* **yourselves.**

(4) 1. I hope you two enjoy .... on your vacation.
  2. I heard you enjoyed .... at the party, Ted.
  3. Is this ...., Ted?
  4. What's the matter with ...., Ted?

VI. *Complete this dialogue. There is more than one "right" answer for each blank.*

  1. —Why are you nervous?   ....
  2. —Which sign?   ....
  3. —But I always turn here.   ....
  4. .... —But I'm only doing 35.
  5. .... —Yes, we have to be there by 5:10.
  6. .... —Why? Do you want to get out?

In this unit we are going to read and talk about the world of fashion.

We are going to study and practice making sentences like these:

What's your jacket **made of?**   Are your socks **made of** nylon?
It's **made of** cotton.   No, they're **made of** wool.

We are also going to use these vocabulary words:

agent	gossiping	sleeveless
announced	hang	sleeves
bargain	loose	special
bathing suit	materials	striking *(adj.)*
canvas	nylon	striped
checked *(adj.)*	outfit	style
collar	pair	suits *(v.)*
collection	pantsuit	tight
combination	patterned	trousers
cotton	plastic	waistlines
cuffs	poetry	wide-bottomed
daring	polka-dot	wide-brimmed
drugstore	respectable	wool
fashionable	rubber	worn
	silk	

WARM-UP

—Where did you buy that hat?
—I bought it at a sale at Bee's.
—How much did you pay for it?
—Oh, believe me, it was a real bargain.
—I must say it really suits you.
—Do you really think so?
—Yes, the color goes well with your eyes.

SMALL TALK

—Look, there's **Ted.**
—I can't see him. What's he wearing?
—The latest thing— **a sleeveless jacket!**

1. **Jim   a striped pantsuit**   2. **Chuck   wide-bottomed trousers**

3. **Chet   a polka-dot shirt**   4. **Roy   a patterned shirt with no collar**

—Do you like my new **bathing suit?**
—Yes, it's very **pretty.**
—You don't think it's too **daring?**
—No, it looks **respectable** enough.

1. **coat**
    elegant
    long
    short

2. **dress**
    nice
    tight
    loose

3. **ski jacket**
    fashionable
    light
    heavy

READ AND UNDERSTAND

Fashion News

Charles of New York showed his spring collection yesterday. This year's colors for both men and women will be yellow and black. A lot of fashionable young men will be upset to hear that hair will be shorter this year. Charles himself prefers the bald look.

Women will wear dresses that hang straight from the neck to the ankle. Pantsuits and waistlines are out! Charles expects that light materials will be most popular. Hats are back again. They're wide-brimmed and bright, but not too big.

Patterns will be popular, especially in checked, striped, and dotted combinations. The most exciting news in men's fashions is wide-bottomed trousers which stop just below the kneecap! Sleeves are out, so jackets will be sleeveless. Shirts will be very daring, in bright colors with no cuffs or collars. Ties are out — scarves are in.

Charles's publicity agent, Gilda Gaybody, just announced today that the president has ordered his first pair of knee-length trousers!

1. What will be the most fashionable colors this year?
2. How will men's hair styles be different?
3. Does Charles prefer to wear his hair long or short?
4. How will trousers be different from the trousers being worn now?
5. Do you think the new fashions will be a success? Why?

STUDY AND PRACTICE

—What's your **jacket** made of?
—It's made of **cotton.**

1. **wool**   2. **silk**   3. **nylon**   4. **plastic**

—What are your **shoes** made of?
—They're made of **leather.**

1. **cotton**   2. **canvas**   3. **rubber**   4. **nylon**

—Are these socks made of nylon?
—No, they're made of wool.

Answer in your own words.

1. Are these trousers made of wool?
2. Is this shirt made of cotton?
3. Are these boots made of leather?
4. Is this raincoat made of canvas?
5. Are those stockings made of nylon?

Two girls are sitting in a drugstore. They are gossiping about Martha's latest boyfriend. Linda is telling Pauline what Martha has said about him, but Pauline already knows all about him!

—Martha said he wore terrific clothes.

—Well, he didn't wear terrific clothes when *I* dated him.

—She said he drove a Jaguar.

—Well, he didn't drive a Jaguar when *I* dated him.

—He bought her flowers every day.

—He didn't buy me flowers when *I* dated him.

—She said he spent hundreds of dollars taking her out.

—He didn't spend hundreds of dollars taking me out when *I* dated him.

—And he read her poetry.

—He didn't read me poetry when *I* dated him.

—And he sang outside her window.

—He didn't sing outside my window when *I* dated him.

—He told her he loved her.

—Ah, yes. He told me loved me when I dated him. He tells all the girls he loves them.

—**Doesn't Mary** look nice in **her** new clothes?
—Yes, they really suit **her.**
—And the colors are just perfect.
—Yes, they go well with **her** hair and eyes.

1. **Jack**
2. **the boys**
3. **I**
4. **we**
5. **you**

—Do you like **Tom's** new clothes?
—I haven't seen **him** wearing them yet.

1. **Elizabeth's**
2. **mother's**
3. **father's**
4. **my**
5. **our**
6. **their**
7. **the boys'**
8. **your parents'**

Tom

Elizabeth

DIALOGUE

Where did you get that | dress? / hat? / ………

I bought it | at a special sale. / at Bee's. / ………………………

How much did it cost?

| It was a real bargain. / Much too much. / ………………dollars. |

| Well, it's different. / It really suits you. |

It's the latest thing.

Really? I like the pattern.

Yes, | checked / dot / striped | patterns are "in."

And the pattern goes so well

with your | eyes! / face! / hair! |

What do you mean by that?

I'm only joking.

What do you think my | wife / husband / mother | will say about it?

Probably that it's very

| fashionable. / daring. / different. |

Well, I like it. Say, have you heard the latest gossip about Gertrude?

No, what's new?

MIXED BAG

The Fashion Show

Charles is wearing a checked, sleeveless jacket and knee-length, wide-bottomed trousers. The most striking part of his outfit is his red and green polka-dot shirt, worn with a silk scarf.

Now describe Francine and Sidney. Add colors of your own to complete their fashionable outfits.

In this unit we are going to read and talk about the world of advertising and the things people buy.

We are going to study and practice making sentences like:

What's the **cheapest** rice?
What's the **least expensive** detergent?

Medicine is sold at a drugstore.
Tools are sold at a hardware store.

We are also going to use these vocabulary words:

advertising	gallon	margarine	sample
afterwards	grocery store	medicine	scissors
ahead	gum	mix-up	seafood
aspirin	hair spray	newsstand	shrimp
brewery	hammer	once	soap
bureau	hardware store	pack (*n.*)	spray
campaign	high-powered	perfume	terrific
confused	ignore	point (*n.*)	tools
compare	least	prefers	toothpaste
department store	lipstick	product	troubles
detergent	loaf (*n.*)	public	tube
fattening	lobster	rice	twice

WARM-UP

—Don't you wash with WAVE?
—Why should I?
—Well, WAVE washes whiter than white, you know!
—You don't say!

—Why don't you buy ENCORE margarine?
—Because my family prefers butter.
—But ENCORE tastes just as good as butter.
—I'm sure I could tell the difference.

SMALL TALK

—What's the **cheapest rice?**
—**Wonder Rice.**
—I've never heard of it.
—You must have. It's sold at every **grocery store.**

1. **best perfume**
   True Love
   department store

2. **most interesting magazine**
   This Week
   newsstand

3. **least fattening margarine**
   Slim
   grocery store

4. **shiniest lipstick**
   Passion
   drugstore

1. What's the most expensive detergent?
2. What's the least fattening margarine?
3. What's the most popular soap?
4. What's the most high-powered radio?
5. What's the least expensive detergent?
6. What can you say about *Wave* detergent?
7. What can you say about *Encore* margarine?
8. What can you say about *Sudsy* soap?
9. What can you say about *Rudy's* radio?

READ AND UNDERSTAND

The Crazy World of Advertising

Not too long ago, a Chicago brewery introduced a new beer that was supposed to be the least fattening on the market. It was lighter, so they called it LITE. Only two months after the new beer had been on sale, however, strange new ads appeared in the Chicago newspapers. They said "LITE TASTES SOAPY."

The public, of course, was confused. Who wanted a beer that tasted like soap—even if it was non-fattening? The new ads weren't talking about LITE beer, however. They were for a product of the Lite Soap Company.

The president of the Lite Soap Company, Mrs. Ruth Ascott, was very upset with the brewery for taking the name of her high-powered detergent and using it as the name of a new beer. Lite Soap had had the same name for 53 years. She wrote to the brewery, insisting that they could not use the word LITE in their beer ads. The brewery replied that they could—and would—because beer and soap were so different. They planned to ignore the "LITE TASTES SOAPY" ads, since the public knew which LITE was which.

Mrs. Ascott was, the last we heard, planning a new campaign. The ads would read "LITE IS WONDERFUL FOR WASHING CLOTHES."

1. Why was LITE supposed to be better than others?
2. How did the new ads say LITE tasted?
3. Why did Mrs. Ascott say the name LITE belonged to her company?
4. Why wasn't the brewery worried about the mix-up in names?
5. Do you think Mrs. Ascott's latest campaign will help beer sales? Why or why not?

STUDY AND PRACTICE

Food			grocery store.
Furniture			department store.
Medicine			drugstore.
Seafood	is	sold at a	fish market.
Newspapers	are		newsstand.
Cars			car dealer's.
Tools			hardware store.

—Where can I buy **margarine?**
—You can buy it at a **grocery store.**

1. **a station wagon**

2. **the New York Times**

3. **lobster**

4. **aspirin**

5. **a bureau**

6. **a hammer**

7. **a refrigerator**

8. **a saw**

9. **shrimp**

—Where can I buy **a can of hair spray?**
—It's either sold at the supermarket or the **drugstore.**

 1. **a tube of lipstick**

 2. **a pack of cigarettes**

 3. **a pound of potatoes**

 4. **a pair of scissors**

 5. **a gallon of paint**

 6. **a bottle of aspirin**

 7. **a box of nails**

 8. **a set of tools**

 9. **a case of coke**

 10. **a loaf of bread**

 11. **a tube of toothpaste**

 12. **a pack of gum**

DIALOGUE

Good morning. Would you answer a few questions

about | WAVE detergent?
ENCORE margarine?

Go ahead and ask.
Hurry up, I've a lot to do.

Have you ever used | WAVE?
ENCORE?

Once or twice.
Yes, often.

What do you think of our product?
Would you like to compare it with others?

It's | the best there is.
just like all the others.

Have you ever thought about the price?

It's so much cheaper.
I never buy it anyway.

But it washes whiter.
But it tastes just like butter.

You don't have to tell me that.
Don't try to tell me that.

We're having a special sale this week.

I'll have another box.
Is it that hard to sell?

It's been a pleasure talking to you.
I can see there's no point in talking to you.

The pleasure was all mine.
I told you I was in a hurry.

Please accept this free

sample of | WAVE
ENCORE.

Thank you.
No, thanks.

MIXED BAG

Look at the pictures on page 56 and answer the following questions.

1. Does the girl sell furniture or groceries?
2. Does she have her lunch in a restaurant, or at home?
3. Does she sit alone, or with friends?
4. Does she have a lot of dances, or very few?
5. Does she walk home, or is she driven home?
6. Does she tell her friend her troubles, or not?
7. Is Spring toothpaste or hair spray?
8. Does she brush her teeth, or comb her hair?
9. Is she popular or not afterwards?
10. Does she take her tube of Spring with her or leave it at home?
11. Does she get married or not?

Write one or two paragraphs about "The Spring Story". Make your story interesting. These questions will help you.

1. What's the girl's name? Describe her.
2. Where does she live?
3. What about her family?
4. How old is she?
5. What is she interested in?

In this unit we are going to read and talk about how people buy things they want or need.

We are going to study and practice making sentences like:

Have you **ordered** the beds?
Yes, I think they've **been ordered.**

Have they **mailed** the order yet?
No, but they know it **must be mailed** today.

When **will** they **mail** the order?
It **will be mailed** later today.

We are also going to use these vocabulary words:

advantage	detail	quit
afford	disadvantages	reasons
amount	down payment	refunded
catalogue	electric	shopper
certain	household goods	size
commission	item	sorted
companies	merchandise	stereo
contain	mail-order	stove
credit	main	total
customers	payments	washing machine
desk	percent	wide-spread
	printed	

WARM-UP

—Dobson's—Order Department.
—My name's Brady. I ordered a bed two months ago,
 and it hasn't been delivered yet.
—I'll check on that.
—And a sweater I bought from you
 has a hole in it.
—Send it back. If our merchandise
 is faulty, your money will be
 refunded.

SMALL TALK

—How much is that **living room set?**
—**$450.** You can put **10 percent** down, and pay the rest on time.
—How much are the monthly payments?
—They're only **$16.**

1. **washing machine**
   $210
   6%
   $12

2. **hair dryer**
   $28.88
   20%
   $5

3. **vacuum cleaner**
   $89.50
   5%
   $11

4. **electric stove**
   $230.75
   10%
   $14

5. **stereo**
   $599.50
   8%
   $25

6. **lawn mower**
   $75
   10%
   $10

READ AND UNDERSTAND

Buying By Mail

You have probably seen ads in newspapers or on TV for mail-order houses. Perhaps you have been sent a catalogue and have bought something by mail. Why do people buy things they have not seen in person? One of the main reasons might be that some people believe that things can be bought more cheaply by mail. Another advantage of mail-order shopping is that it is more comfortable to sit at home and look through a catalogue than to rush around the stores. With a catalogue from a large firm, you have your own shop window for almost everything you might want to buy.

The mail-order business is very wide-spread. Some companies have agents who show merchandise from the catalogues to likely customers. Perhaps you have had one of these agents call you or come by your home. They are paid a commission for every order they take.

Buying from a catalogue is so easy. It saves the shopper time and trouble. Sometimes, it saves the shopper money on one item. But people often buy more than they can really afford, since they can buy on time, or credit. Some companies allow a customer to pay for an item over a long period of time if they have a charge account. People can also pay a certain percent of the total price. This is called a down payment. Then the customer pays a certain amount of money every month until the merchandise is completely paid for. Mail-order houses sell just about everything—furniture, tools, household goods—even heavy machinery and vehicles.

1. How do mail-order houses advertise?
2. What are the advantages of buying by mail?
3. What are the disadvantages of buying by mail?
4. What is the difference between charging an item and paying for it on time?

STUDY AND PRACTICE

—Have you **ordered the beds?**
—Yes, I think **they've been ordered.**

1. **delivered the dryers**
2. **paid the bill**
3. **sent the packages**
4. **fixed the washing machines**
5. **sorted the mail**
6. **ordered the stereo**

—I'd like to buy some **furniture**, but I can't afford it.
—Well, **chairs** can be bought on time, you know.

—Have they **mailed the letter** yet? — No, but they know it must be **mailed** today.

1. delivered the order   delivered
2. printed the catalogue   printed
3. fixed the lawn mower   fixed
4. sent the package   sent
5. sorted the mail   sorted
6. paid the bill   paid

—When will they **mail the letter**? — It will be **mailed later today.**

1. deliver the order   delivered before noon
2. print the catalogue   printed in January
3. fix the lawn mower   fixed next week
4. send the package   sent at two o'clock
5. sort the mail   sorted tomorrow
6. pay the bill   paid next month

What are they saying?

Maria Rodrigo works very hard at the office. Her boss never thinks she is busy enough, however. Every morning, he asks her what she did the day before.

— Did you check the catalogues?

— Yes sir. They were checked last night.

— Did you call for the latest reports?

— Yes sir. They were called for last night.

— Did you type all the letters?

— Yes sir. They were typed last night.

— Did you pay the bills?

— Yes sir. They were paid last night.

— Did you send the packages?

— Yes sir. They were sent last night.

— Did you deliver the phone orders?

— Yes sir. They were delivered last night.

— Did you order the new furniture?

— Yes sir. It was ordered last night.

— Did you sort the mail?

— Yes sir. It was sorted last night.

— Well, what have you done this morning?

— Cleaned out my desk. I quit!

DIALOGUE

How do you like my new
dishwasher?

Where did you buy it?

> At Star's.
> From the Happy Homes
>   Catalogue.

> I never shop at that store.
> I don't shop by mail.

Why not?

> I like to see what
>   I'm buying.
> Their prices are too high.

> Oh, well, I charged it.
> But the catalogue is just
>   filled with bargains.

> How much of a bargain
>   was it?
> It costs more when you
>   charge it.

> Yes, but I pay only a
>   little each month.
> It was only $139.00.

Well, I'll never have one.

Why not?

> My husband Hank says we
>   can't afford it.
> I don't have a charge
>   account at Star's.

But don't you hate doing
  dishes every day?

Yes, that's why Hank
  does them!

MIXED BAG

Pretend you have bought some clothes from a mail-order company. The package you received in the mail did not contain what you ordered from the catalogue. Write a letter to the manager of the company. Tell him what is wrong with your order, and tell him how upset you are about the poor service. The following sentences will help you write your letter.

1. Tell him what you ordered—describe the clothes in detail.
2. Tell him when you sent the order.
3. How long did it take for the package to arrive?
4. What's wrong with the clothes? Is the color wrong? The size? The pattern?
5. Is your bill correct?
6. Do you want your money back, or a new order?
7. Will you ever shop by mail again? Why or why not?

What's the Word?

1. You may use a .... after you've washed your hair.
2. If the grass has grown too tall, you need to use the ....
3. I make great meals with my new ....
4. My new .... uses less detergent than my old one.
5. Can I play a record on your new ....?
6. Please help me clean. You can do the rugs with the ....
7. My new .... doesn't get glasses very clean.
8. The garage needs painting. Please buy a .... of paint at the .... store.
9. Please pick up some fruit at the .... store on your way home.
10. I need a .... of aspirin from the ....

In this unit we are going to read and talk about emergency situations and how to get help.

We are going to study and practice making sentences with:

who — He's the **one who** . . .
that — It's the **one that** . . .
where — That's **where**. . .

We are also going to use these vocabulary words:

ambulance	medical	protected
damaged	notice (*v.*)	reward
directory	occur	roadblock
easy	operated	roof
emergency	operator	sinking
engine	phrases	situation
fire department	poisonous	squad car
horn	prison	woke

WARM-UP

—Operator, this is an emergency.
  Get me the police!
—Police Department.
—Send a squad car and an ambulance
  to 15 Park Drive right away.
—What's the trouble?
—My cat is on the roof,
  and he can't get down!

—Get me the Fire Department, quick!
—Fire Station Number 3.
—Come quick. We're on fire.
—Have you called the police?
—We *are* the police. The station's on fire!

READ AND UNDERSTAND

Emergency Calls

You may never be part of an emergency situation, but you should know how to get help if one does occur. The telephone company in the United States prints emergency numbers on the inside front cover of the telephone book. This is what the page in the Boston directory looks like.

EMERGENCY NUMBERS

FIRE

BOSTON	911
BROOKLINE	911
CAMBRIDGE	876-5800
SOMERVILLE	623-1500
Other Places	....
	(write in your number here)

POLICE

BOSTON	911
BROOKLINE	911
CAMBRIDGE	864-1212
SOMERVILLE	625-1212
Other Places	....
	(write in your number here)

DOCTOR

(Boston Emergency Physicians Service)	
BOSTON BROOKLINE	482-5252
(Middlesex South District Medical Society)	
CAMBRIDGE SOMERVILLE	625-4774
Other Places	....
	(write in ; our number here)

AMBULANCE .... (write in your number here)   DOCTOR (Personal) .... (write in your doctor's number here)

COAST GUARD .... 223-6978 (Search and Rescue)   POISON .... 232-2120 (Information Center)

F. B. I. .... 742-5533 (Federal Bureau of Investigation)   RESCUE, Inc. .... 426-6600 (Devoted to the prevention of suicide)

⭐ U.S. SECRET SERVICE   223-2728

OR DIAL "0" - OPERATOR IN ANY EMERGENCY,
WE ARE ALWAYS THERE AND READY TO HELP!!
IF you cannot stay at the telephone, give the operator your city or town as well as your street and number, or the exact location where help is needed.

Notice that the number for the police and fire departments is the same, and that it is an easy number to remember. If you are too upset or excited to remember any numbers at all, however, you can simply dial "0" for operator in any emergency.

1. What number would you dial if you saw a fire?
2. What number would you dial if a child had drunk something poisonous?
3. What number would you dial if you saw a boat sinking?
4. What should you tell the operator if you dial "0?"

STUDY AND PRACTICE

—Do you know that **doctor**?
—Yes, **he's** the one who showed me around the **hospital**.

1. **fireman**   **fire station**
2. **policeman**   **police station**
3. **nurse**   **medical school**
4. **ambulance driver** **emergency room**

—Do you recognize the **squad car**?
—Yes, it's the one that was parked **outside the prison**.

1. **in front of the hospital**

3. **on the bridge**

2. **inside the fire station**

4. **in front of the hotel**

—Is that the **police station?**
—Yes, that's where the **thieves** were taken.

(The phrases below are mixed up. Find the correct pairs, and then use them in the dialogue.)

1. **fire station**   **my mother was operated on**
2. **hospital**   **I studied medicine**
   ?   **I bought my new uniform**
3. **medical school**
4. **prison**   **the fire engines are kept**
5. **department store**   **the thieves escaped from**

—The police set up a roadblock here.
—So this is where they set up the roadblock.

1. The police arrested the thieves here.
2. The Fire Department used to have a station here.
3. The medical school used to have a hospital here.
4. The ambulance service had an emergency phone here.

—The police saved that old man.
—So that's who the police saved.

1. The car hit that little boy.
2. The Fire Department rewarded that girl.
3. The police protected that man.
4. The bus knocked down that pedestrian.

—There's the car that crashed into the wall.
—So that's what crashed into the wall.

1. There's the fire engine that delayed the traffic.
2. There's the car that damaged the motorcycle.
3. There's the ambulance that woke you up.
4. There's the truck that broke through the roadblock.

DIALOGUE

Police Department.

Somebody's robbing the bank!
Somebody's downstairs!

Your name and address? ....

....

What number are you calling from? .... Hurry!

Are the thieves still inside? Are you sure somebody's downstairs?	Of course I'm sure. No, they're coming out.

Are they on foot? Were your doors locked?	They're running to a car. Yes, and the windows, too.

A squad car will be right over. Can you see the license number?	No, it's too dark. Hurry! He's climbing out the kitchen window.

Which way are they driving? What's he wearing?	North, toward South Street. Dark clothes, and a mask.

What was that noise?

They just hit a bus.
He just fell over the trash!

Is anyone hurt? Is he hurt?

Yes, better send an ambulance.

I'll call the emergency squad.

MIXED BAG

Read the following description of an accident.

At ten o'clock this morning I was at the drugstore. I was buying a bottle of aspirin and a can of hair spray. Suddenly I heard a car horn. I looked out and saw a blue station wagon speeding down South Street. It was going at least sixty miles an hour. The driver was on the left side of the street. The traffic lights were red, but he didn't stop. He crashed into another car. The driver of the station wagon jumped out and ran down King's Street. He was a tall, thin man with blond hair.

Now write a story of your own. The questions below will help you.

1. Where were you at ten o'clock?
2. What were you doing?
3. What did you hear?
4. What did you do then?
5. What did you see?
6. How fast was the car going?
7. Which side of the street was it on?
8. Were the traffic lights red or green?
9. What did the car crash into?
10. What did the driver do?
11. What did the driver look like?

The Wonderland

| brewery |
| clothing store |
| hardware store |

is planning

an advertising

| campaign |
| company |
| pattern |

to sell their new

| soap. |
| fashions. |
| vehicles. |

The latest

| waistline |
| collection |
| shoulders |

has many

| daring |
| slim |
| wide-bottomed |

patterns

in beautiful colors. The

| boyfriend |
| success |
| agent |

of Wonderland, Larry King,

said that

| hair |
| legs |
| arms |

would be

| larger |
| looser |
| shorter |

to go with the new hats.

Larry himself is

| striped |
| bald |
| dotted |

so he has no problem there.

Wonderland's clothes are

| early |
| easy |
| upset |

to wash in any

| department. |
| detergent. |
| suit. |

II. *What did she buy?*

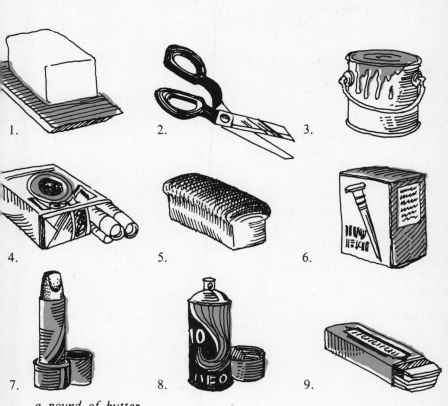

1.

2.

3.

4.

5.

6.

7.

8.

9.

a pound of butter

1. ....
2. ....
3. ....
4. ....
5. ....
6. ....
7. ....
8. ....
9. ....

III.

(5)
1. What did he wear?   He .... fabulous clothes.
2. What did he drive?   He .... a Jaguar.
3. What did he buy?   He .... some flowers.

IV. *Fill in with* **buy, buys,** *or* **bought.**

(6)
1. Food can be .... at a supermarket.
2. The Dobsons are going to .... a new house.
3. Many cars are .... on time.
4. Some people like to .... from mail-order firms.
5. My fathers always .... from such a firm.

V. *Fill in with* **deliver, delivers,** *or* **delivered.**

(7)
1. When will they .... the mail?
2. It has just been ....
3. The mailman often .... it at ten o'clock.
4. Yesterday it was .... at nine.

VI. *Fill in with* **who, what,** *or* **where.**

(8)
1. That's the place .... the thieves were taken.
2. That's the man .... was arrested.
3. That's .... was stolen.
4. That's .... they crashed into the wall.
5. That's .... they told the police.
6. That's the driver .... was hurt.

In this unit we are going to read and talk about our changing world and how "things aren't the way they used to be."

We are going to study and practice making sentences like:

Do you usually **walk** to school?
No, but I **used to walk** last year.

Didn't you **use to walk** there?
No, I **used to go** by car.

We are also going to use these vocabulary words:

architects	hitchhiking	rocky
brand-new	nonsense	seat covers
cemetery	nowadays	set
center	oversleep	thick
confident	promise	unbelievable
disturb	rear-view mirror	whenever
flat (tire)	replace	windshield wipers
ghosts	repaired	wished

WARM-UP

—Hi, Sam. Why are you hitchhiking?
—My car's in the garage again.
—You've really had a lot of trouble with that car.
—Yes, they don't make cars like they used to.
—I thought you had decided to buy a new one.
—I had, but it was too expensive.

SMALL TALK

—This **street** was very **quiet** ten years ago.
—Yes, but now it's very **noisy.**

1. **store**
   small
   large

2. **town**
   dull
   exciting

3. **park**
   clean
   dirty

4. **car**
   cheap
   expensive

5. **catalogue**
   thin
   thick

READ AND UNDERSTAND

My First Car

When I was a teen-ager, we lived out in the country. If we wanted to go to town, we had to walk.

Then I got my first car. I'll never forget it. My father was away in Dallas at the time. I decided to surprise him and meet him with the car. I knew that he expected me to carry his luggage all the way home. My mother didn't want me to drive to town. I had driven it only once before, and wasn't a very confident driver. Besides, she was afraid of what my father would say when he saw the new car. She wanted me to walk to the station and tell him about the car later. But I wanted to show everybody my brand-new car—so off I went.

The train arrived at 3:20. Surprisingly enough, my father wasn't angry when he saw the car. I told him I wasn't a very good driver yet. He said he would be only too pleased to show me how to drive. That really surprised *me*. As far as I knew, my father had never driven a car before.

By the time we got home, I wished I had walked to town. I'm sure my father did, too. The ride home was unbelievable. It was years before my father ever drove again! Whenever the subject was mentioned, he used to reply, "The motor car will never replace the horse."

1. Where did the author live when he was a teen-ager?
2. How did he usually get to town?
3. How did he decide to surprise his father?
4. What did his mother think of the idea?
5. Why did his mother feel that way?
6. Who drove the car home?
7. What do you think happened on the way home?

STUDY AND PRACTICE

It's a dark, windy night in the middle of November. Two men are standing at bus stop by a cemetery.

—Hi, George. I haven't seen you for ages!

—Why don't we have lunch soon? I usually eat at the Crown Restaurant.

—How about a drink, then?

—Do you have any cigarettes?

—How about some tennis this weekend? You used to be good.

—Hmmmm. You're not enjoying life like you used to, George.

—What? What do you mean?

—I know that bus is late. I catch it right at 9.

—What do you mean? That bus goes right by where I live.

—Nonsense! I'm not ready to die. And I don't believe in ghosts.

—I haven't been too well lately.

—I used to go there, too. But don't have the time nowad

—Sorry. I used to drink, but had to give it up.

—Sorry. I used to smoke, but had to give it up.

—Sorry. I had to give it up.

—You're right. I gave it up.

—Poor Henry. You don't know what's happened, do you?

—You mean "used to catch," Henry. You'll never ride th bus again.

—You mean "used to live." Henry, you died this afternoon. You're a ghost. I'm a ghost, too!

—You'll get used to the idea.

> —Do you usually **walk to school**?
> —No, but I used to **walk to school** last year.

1. **ride a bike to school**
2. **work at home**
3. **go to bed at nine**
4. **have a big breakfast**
5. **work overtime**
6. **play golf on Saturdays**
7. **catch the bus to work**
8. **have lunch here**
9. **hitchhike to the beach**

> —Didn't you use to **walk** there?
> —No, I used to go by **car**.

1. **ride your bike**

2. **hitchhike**

3. **fly**

4. **drive**

—Have you talked about buying **a new car**?
—Yes, but we decided not to.

1. **new windshield wipers**

2. **a set of tires**

3. **a radio**

4. **a rear-view mirror**

5. **a set of seat covers**

—Why did he go to the **train station?**
—He went there to buy **a ticket.**

1. **hardware store**

2. **newsstand**

3. **drugstore**

4. **cafeteria**

—What did he say about **fixing the flat tire**?
—Oh, he was happy to **fix it**.

1. **refunding the money**
2. **washing the car**
3. **fixing the horn**
4. **paying for the tickets**
5. **ordering the seat covers**

—I'll never **smoke** again.
—Is that a promise?
—Yes, I promise never to **smoke** again.

1. **drive fast**
2. **drink**
3. **disturb you**
4. **steal**
5. **be late**
6. **oversleep**

DIALOGUE

Hello! Aren't you . . .?
Excuse me. Don't I know you?

I don't believe it! It's . . .
Hello! What a coincidence.

You haven't changed a bit.
You look the same as always.

Neither have you.
So do you.

How long has it been?
It must be 20 years since we
last met.

Yes, at least.
At least twenty years.

Do you still live in town?

Yes, in the same old house.
No, I'm just visiting.

I'm just passing through.

The town doesn't look like
it used to, does it?

You can say that again.
No, I'd hardly recognize it.

There are many new buildings.
The center of town is all new.

I miss the big old houses.
The new buildings are ugly.

They don't build houses like
they used to.
Architects today have some
strange ideas.

I suppose you're right.

Remember when we had to

walk a mile to school?
shop in the next town?

Things have really changed,
but I still have to walk.

Why, don't you own a car?

Yes, but it's being repaired
again.

They don't make cars like they
used to.
Some things never change.

MIXED BAG

What do you have to do?

1. Your car is dirty.
2. You run out of gas.
3. You get a flat.
4. You're speeding.
5. You're driving and it gets dark.
6. You're driving and you want to listen to some music.
7. You get a parking ticket.
8. You're driving to a place you've never been to before.
9. You come to a stop sign.
10. You're driving and it starts to rain.

Odd Man Out

1. a gallon, a bottle, a can, a stove
2. customer, store, ghost, salesman
3. credit, fattening, cash, charge
4. rice, lobster, margarine, detergent
5. aspirin, saw, hammer, nails
6. dishwasher, stove, stereo, washing machine
7. squad car, replace, ambulance, fire engine
8. horn, windshield wipers, cemetery, seat covers
9. drive, oversleep, hitchhike, fly
10. nonsense, operator, directory, telephone

In this unit we are going to read and talk about ways to travel —
especially by train.

We are going to study and practice making sentences like:

What should I write?
Sorry, I don't know what to write either.
Would you **like** a new racket?
No thanks. **I would** rather keep my old one.

You **can** stop now.
I said that you **could** stop now.

Are you sure he **will** go by train?
I'm not sure, but he said he **might.**

We are also going to use these vocabulary words:

ceremony	locomotive
change *(money)*	map
coaches	matches
conventional	panicked
direct *(adj.)*	pardon
double	parlor
either	schedule
expected	seems
fear *(n.)*	steam
froze	track

WARM-UP

—When is the train from Pittsburgh due?
— At 10:27.
— What track?
— Either nine or ten.

— Is the 9:40 to Detroit delayed?
— That's right.
— How late will it be?
— It was due at 9:20, but now it's not expected until 9:45.

READ AND UNDERSTAND

Opening Day on the Railroad

The first public railroad in the world to be run by steam was opened in England in 1825. It was a single track. The next big railroad was a double track that ran between Manchester and Liverpool. The opening day was a great success—except for Mr. Huskisson, that is.

Eight trains took part in the opening ceremony. There were 600 people in 29 coaches. After traveling for 17 miles, the trains had to stop for water. Mr. Huskisson got out of his train to talk to a friend on one of the other trains. He was half-way across the track when he suddenly saw a locomotive racing toward him. It was going at a fantastic speed—23 miles per hour! Mr. Huskisson panicked and froze with fear. He was run over by the train, and died the same evening.

1. What happened in 1825?
2. How was the second railroad different from the first?
3. Why did the trains stop after 17 miles?
4. Why did Mr. Huskisson get off the train?
5. Why didn't he move when he saw the locomotive coming?

STUDY AND PRACTICE

—What should I write?
—I'm sorry. I can't help you.
—Why not?
—I don't know what to write either.

1. What should I say?
2. What should I tell her?
3. Where should I begin?
4. Where should I get off?
5. How should I behave?
6. How should I answer?
7. When should I leave?
8. When should I get up?

—I think he's a good teacher.
—Do you really think so?
—Yes, he seems to be a good
   teacher.

1. I think he's a good driver.
2. I think he enjoys himself.
3. I think he's an excellent student.
4. I think it's too warm in here.
5. I think the time passes quickly.

—Would you like a new **racket**?
—No thanks. I'd rather keep my old one.

1.

5.

2.

6.

3.

7.

4.

8.

—He's a good **talker**, isn't he?
—I don't know. I can never make him **talk**.

1. **singer**
   sing

2. **painter**
   paint

3. **player**
   play

4. **dancer**
   dance

5. **actor**
   act

6. **writer**
   write

—You can **stop** now.
—Pardon?
—I said that you could **stop** now.

1. go
2. open the window
3. close the door
4. rest
5. leave
6. sit down

—Are you sure he'll **go by train?**
—I'm not sure, but he said he might.

1. drive   2. take a plane   3. ride his bike

4. walk   5. go by boat   6. hitchhike

—I can't find my **money.**
—You'd better look in your **wallet.**

1. **ticket**

desk

2. **map**

car

3. **keys**

pocket

4. **matches**

purse

5. **papers**

briefcase

6. **jewelry**

bureau

—It's **late.**
—Yes, we'd better **go home** now.

1. **dark**   Yes, we'd better turn on the lights now.
2. **cold**   Yes, we'd better . . .
3. **hot**
4. **raining**
5. **early**

DIALOGUE

When is the next train to Erie?

At . . . .

Is it direct, or do I have to change?

There are no direct trains.
You have to change.
There's a direct train tonight.

Where do I have to change?
I'll take the evening train.

Okay.
In Buffalo.

How much is it?

One-way?

Yes.
No, round-trip.

That's thirty dollars
Fifty-nine dollars.

Which track will it be?

Track Nine.
Look at the schedule.

Will it be on time?

Yes, it's due in five minutes.
No, it's been delayed.

I have time to eat, then.
I'd better hurry.

Hey! Come back.

What's the matter?

You haven't paid me.
You forgot your change.

MIXED BAG

Below is part of a train schedule. Study the information shown carefully, and then answer the questions.

NEW YORK — WASHINGTON, D.C.

	New York Penn. Sta. Leave	Philadelphia (Penn Central Sta.) Leave	Washington Arrive
167 The Night Owl *(Monday-Thursday)*	4:20 am	6:05	8:30 am
101 Metroliner *(daily)*	7:30 am	8:46	10:34 am
103 Metroliner *(Mondays thru Thursdays)*	8:30 am	9:48	11:34 am
173 The Minute Man *(daily, except Sunday)*	4:45 pm	6:16	8:23 pm
182 The Senator *(daily)*	7:30 pm	9:13	11:20 pm
186 Metroliner *(daily)*	8:30 pm	9:43	11:30 pm

ONE-WAY FARES (Double for round-trip)

Between	In Metroliner Coaches	In Regular Coaches
New York and		
Trenton	$6.50	$3.50
Philadelphia	8.25	5.25
Baltimore	9.50	5.50
Washington	18.50	11.25

1. What is the earliest train to Washington? What time does it arrive?
2. What time does **The Senator** stop in Philadelphia?
3. What time does **The Minute Man** leave New York?
4. Would you take the **103 Metroliner** if you wanted arrive in Washington early on a Sunday morning?
5. Would you take **The Minute Man** if you wanted to meet a friend in Philadelphia for lunch?
6. How much is a one-way ticket between New York and Philadelphia by **Metroliner** coach? By regular coach?
7. How much is a round-trip ticket between New York and Washington by regular coach? By **Metroliner** coach?

In this unit we are going to read and talk about the police and their work.

We are going to study and practice making sentences like:

What does Tom want to do?   He wants **to watch** TV.
What's Tom looking forward   He's looking forward **to**
   to doing?   **watching** TV.

I drove home without **being stopped.**
Oh, didn't anybody **stop** you?

How many times did he **ask** you?
He **asked** me again and again.
He just kept **asking** me.

We are also going to use these vocabulary words:

clues	gang
controls *(n.)*	obviously
creeping	out of order
disappeared	rest rooms
disconnected	stamp
fingerprints	suitable
five-pound notes	unloaded
forward	warning
	worth

WARM-UP

—The police kept stopping me on my way home tonight.
—I guess they're looking for that hold-up gang.
—There were road blocks everywhere.
—I drove home without being stopped.
—You were just lucky.

SMALL TALK

—Where's the nearest **telephone,** please?
—It's **next to the rest rooms.**

1. service station   at the bottom of the hill

2. bank   beside the library

3. train station   at the end of the street

4. ticket window   at the foot of the stairs

5. stamp machine   inside the drugstore

6. coffee shop   opposite the traffic lights

READ AND UNDERSTAND

The Great Train Robbery

At 3 a.m. on August the 8th, Jack Mills was sitting at the controls of the mail train from Glasgow to London. The train was made up of 13 coaches. At the end of the train, 71 mailmen sat sorting the mail. Inside the second coach, there were only five mailmen—and 128 bags full of five-pound notes! This train had run more than 100 years without being robbed.

At three minutes past three, Mills and his helper, David Whitby, saw a yellow warning light. They slowed the train, and then stopped. Whitby went to the telephone beside the track. It was out of order. Then he saw a man creeping between the second and third coaches. Before Whitby could give a warning, he was knocked down by two men.

Mills was ordered to drive the train to a bridge that crossed a road. The last ten coaches with all the mailmen had been disconnected by the robbers. At the bridge, the bags of money were unloaded from the train and thrown into waiting trucks. One of the robbers who obviously knew the schedules of all the trains kept looking at his watch.

At 3:45 he said, That will have to be enough." The robbers escaped with more then £ 2,500,000!

1. What were the 71 men at the end of the train doing?
2. Why did Jack Mills stop the train?
3. Why was it impossible to telephone for help?
4. What did the robbers do with the moneybags?
5. Why do you think they had to stop at 3:45?
6. How much is £ 2,500,000 worth in the money of your country?

STUDY AND PRACTICE

What does Tom want to do? What's Tom looking forward to doing?	He wants to **watch TV.** He's looking forward to **watching TV.**

1.

2.

3.

4.

5.

6.

7.

8.

9.

10.

11.

12.

—I drove home without being stopped.
—Oh, didn't anybody stop you?

1. I came here without being seen.
2. I learned English without being taught.
3. I agreed to sing without being paid.
4. I cleaned my room without being told to.
5. I sat in class without being questioned.

—Did anybody stop you when you drove home?
—No, I drove home without being stopped.

1. Did anybody see you when you came here?
2. Did anybody teach you when you learned English?
3. Did anybody pay you when you sang?
4. Did anybody tell you to clean when you cleaned your room?
5. Did anybody question you when you sat in class?

> —How many times did he **ask you?**
> —He **asked me** again and again.
> —Really?
> —Yes, he just kept **asking me.**

1. **hit you** (hit, hitting)
2. **ring the bell** (rang, ringing)
3. **steal the ball** (stole, stealing)
4. **escape from prison** (escaped, escaping)
5. **fight with Tom** (fought, fighting)

Complete these sentences in your own words. Use the -ing forms.

1. I enjoy....................................
2. I dislike..................................
3. I don't mind...................................
4. I read about a man who was arrested for ....
5. I left home this morning without...................................

Complete these sentences with suitable words.

1. My best friend.................going to the movies.
2. I.................speaking English as often as I can.
3. My father.................paying too much for food last year.
4. Our teacher.................giving us too much homework last year.
5. He.................the ball three times.
6. The bell kept.................and.................
7. Did he often.................Jane for a date?
8. Yes, he just kept.................and.................her.
9. I cleaned my room without.................told to.
10. She sang .... paid.
11. I drove home without ....

DIALOGUE

Did you hear about the robbery?

No, which one?
Where was it?
You mean the one downtown?

Yes, the one at the bank.
At the post office.
At the jewelry store.

How did they get in?
Did they rob it at night?

No, during lunch time.
Through the back door.

Have they found any clues?
Didn't anybody see them?

A few fingerprints.
No, they were very careful.

Do you think they'll be caught?

Only if they're careless.
The fingerprints might help.

Being a policeman is a hard job.
A policeman stopped me last week.

What for?
You can say that again.

Speeding!
But they're never around when you need them.

Do you have time for coffee?

Thanks, but I don't.

Where are you rushing off to?

To the bank. I'm taking out my money!

MIXED BAG

On Wednesday morning at eleven o'clock, I was walking down Main Street. I had just parked my car. Suddenly I heard two shots! I thought they had come from the bank. I ran toward the bank. I saw a man coming out. He was short and fat with a big moustache. More important, he had a bag of money and a gun in his hands! Before I could do anything, he ran up the street and disappeared behind a bus. That afternoon I went to the movies. I saw the thief again at the foot of the stairs! I telephoned the police from a telephone next to the rest rooms. The police arrived in less than five minutes. They arrested the thief just as he was buying a chocolate bar from the candy machine! What an exciting day! And best of all, the bank gave me a $100 reward!

Now write a story of your own. The questions below will help you.

1. What day was it?
2. What time was it?
3. What had you just done?
4. What did you suddenly hear?
5. Where did you run to?
6. What did you see?
7. What did the thief look like?
8. What did he have in his hands?
9. How did he escape?
10. What did you do that afternoon?
11. Where did you see the thief again?
12. What did you do then?
13. What was the thief doing when the police arrested him?
14. How much was your reward?

In this unit we are going to read and talk about people's ambitions —the jobs they want to have, things they want to enjoy, etc.

We are going to study and practice making sentences like these:

My brother doesn't have **any** money.
Why don't you lend him **some?**

Bill doesn't have a pen.
Can't he **borrow** one from Wendy?
No, she doesn't have one to **lend** him.

She's **doing** me a favor.
He's **doing** his homework.

Rich men **make** money.
Poor students **make** mistakes.

We are also going to use these vocabulary words:

agree	employment	impression	prove
ambitious	energetic	investing	reassure
announcer	engineer	judges	rescue
astronaut	extra	lawyer	route
borrowed	favor	lend	sandstorm
childhood	female	lent	script
common	failing	mechanic	unfortunately
decisions	fortune	monsoon	university
dentist	habit	management	unusual
diseases	hire	politicians	veterinarian
electrician	human	propeller	

—What would you like to do most of all?
—Fly to the moon. What about you?
—I'd like to make a fortune.
—The best way to do that is by investing your money.
—I agree. Can you lend me ten dollars?

SMALL TALK

—What would you like to be?
—I'd like to be **a pilot.**
—You'd be good at that.

1. **a TV announcer**

2. **an astronaut**

3. **a dentist**

4. **a veterinarian**

5. **an architect**

6. **a lawyer**

7. **an engineer**

8. **a mechanic**

9. **an electrician**

READ AND UNDERSTAND

An Unusual Woman

Amy Johnson was a very ambitious and energetic person. She didn't have much in common with other girls in her school, however. She played football better than most boys, and unfortunately, she made a rather bad impression on many of her teachers. Amy just didn't act the way they thought a girl should. She studied at a university and later took a job as a typist. Although she was enthusiastic and did her best, she made many mistakes and was poorly paid. She didn't want to be a typist anyway—she dreamed of becoming a pilot!

Amy moved to London, borrowed some money, and learned to fly. Nobody, however, wanted to hire a female pilot. She decided to fly alone to Australia to prove that she could fly as well as any man. Her parents lent her money to buy an airplane.

Amy set off on May 5, 1930. Her route took her over Vienna, Constantinople, and Baghdad. She was caught in a sandstorm and had to make an emergency landing in the desert. But she landed in India six days later. She had broken the record to India by two days. Over Burma she ran into a monsoon, and was able to save herself only by landing on a football field. She finally reached Australia. The plane propeller had been broken during her last landing, and she had to crash-land. But Amy had proven that she could fly—and that a woman could do most anything she really put her mind to.

Amy Johnson later married the pilot who had come to her rescue in Australia.

1. Why didn't many of the teachers like Amy?
2. Why wasn't she a very successful typist?
3. Who lent her the money to buy a plane?
4. Why did she have to land in the desert?
5. Why did she land in a football field?
6. How did Amy meet her husband?

STUDY AND PRACTICE

Borrow and lend.

—My brother doesn't have any money.
—Why don't you lend him some?
—I don't have any either.

1. My father doesn't have any books.
2. My mother doesn't have any lipstick.
3. You don't have any stamps.
4. Tom and his sister don't have any towels.
5. You don't have any tools.

—Bill doesn't have a pen, but Wendy has.
—Can't he borrow one from her?
—No. She doesn't have an extra one to lend him.

1. Harry doesn't have a tie, but Bill has.
2. Marty doesn't have a sweater, but Amy has.
3. Alice doesn't have a pen, but Hank has.
4. Aki doesn't have a pencil, but Sybil has.
5. Sara doesn't have a racket, but they have.

Fill in with either **borrow** *or* **lend.**

1. I can't find my book. I'll have to .... one from Tom.
2. Can you .... me some money?
3. Why don't you .... me money, since you just got paid?
4. Never .... Jack anything — you'll never get it back!
5. Can I .... your car tonight?
6. Did you .... these books from the library?
7. Please .... me a dollar until tomorrow.
8. I really don't like to .... people money.
9. Did you .... my racket to Sue?
10. Jack wants to .... some tools from us.

> —What's he doing?
> —**He's** doing **nothing at all.**

1. What's she doing?   some housework for her mother
2. What's mother doing?   the dishes
3. What's Harry doing?   silly things, as usual
4. What's father doing?   business with Mr. Monk
5. What's Sheila doing?   her homework
6. What's Randy doing?   me a favor

> —What do rich men do?
> —**Rich men** make **money.**

1. What do poor students do?   many mistakes
2. What do clever girls do?   good impressions
3. What do smokers do?   a habit of smoking
4. What do politicians do?   speeches
5. What do judges do?   decisions
6. What do people who try hard do?   an effort

Fill in with the correct forms of **do** *or* **make.**

1. He is very successful. He .... a lot of business with Japan.
2. Tom is failing chemistry. I wish he would .... an effort.
3. It's a bad idea to .... a habit of smoking.
4. Rock musicians .... a lot of money.
5. Mother is .... the dishes.
6. You need to study more. You .... too many mistakes.
7. Can you .... me a favor?
8. I'll .... the extra work if you don't have time.
9. Bill always .... a bad impression.
10. She stays in bed on Sundays. She .... nothing at all!

DIALOGUE

Let's hear your first line.
Have you learned the script?

Hi! My name's Kim Kent.
Yes, I have.

Again, with a big smile.
Let's do it with no mistakes.

Hi! My name's Kim Kent.
I'll try not to make any.

That's better. Look
  enthusiastic.
Look a little sad.

Have you tried new *Spring?*
I used to have bad breath.

Whisper the next line.
Be serious now.

I was very upset.
Spring polishes your teeth
  like no other product can.

Now a big, confident smile.
Tell them who makes it.

It's made by Bing Brothers.
Then *Spring* changed my
  whole life.

Tell about the price.

Spring costs only 98¢ a tube.
Spring is on sale now for
  just 79¢.

Look enthusiastic again.
Reassure them now.

It really *will* change your life.
Spring makes your breath
  sweet and your teeth super
  white.

Okay, show them the ring.
Okay, end with the question.

Can you afford *not* to use
  Spring?
And *Spring* got me this!

That sounds great.
Let's film it.

MIXED BAG

Occupations

1. Pete is a jet pilot. Which of the following things do you think are important for him in his job? Why?
   a. geography
   b. sales reports
   c. weather patterns
   d. typing
   e. mechanical engineering
   f. air traffic reports

2. Sally is in her last year of medical school. Which of the following do you think she would be most interested in? Why?
   a. childhood diseases
   b. office management
   c. parts of the body
   d. chemistry
   e. typing
   f. geography

3. Randy is a lawyer. Which of the following would he be most interested in? Why?
   a. weather patterns
   b. police reports
   c. human behavior
   d. law books
   e. sales reports
   f. prisons

4. Martha is a new reporter on a newspaper. Which of the following would she need to know a lot about? Why?
   a. human behavior
   b. police reports
   c. mechanical engineering
   d. English
   e. sales reports
   f. chemistry

5. Jack is an ambitious salesman who wants to become president of his company one day. Which of the following would Jack spend a lot of time on? Why?
   a. chemistry
   b. sales reports
   c. office management
   d. human behavior
   e. employment laws
   f. air traffic reports

TEST YOURSELF

I.

1. The opening day was a t .... success.
2. When he saw the train, he p ...., and couldn't move.
3. He was k .... down and killed by a train.
4. I usually keep my money in my w ....
5. The mailmen sat in the last ten c .... of the train.
6. The train stopped at a b .... over a road.
7. One of the men o .... knew when the train was due.
8. The robbers e .... with one million dollars.
9. The police found the robber's f .... on the door and desk.
10. A doctor studies for many years in m .... s ....
11. The man got a r .... of $50 when he found the jewelry.

II. *Complete this dialogue at the train station.*

1. ....? —It leaves for Washington at 9:45.
2. ....? —It arrives at 12:20.
3. ....? —Twenty-four dollars.
4. ....? —That's one-way.
5. ....? —No, it's delayed.

III. *Fill in with* **eat, to eat, eating, eats, ate,** *or* **eaten.**

(9, 10)
1. I think he .... too much nowadays.
2. He has decided not .... so much.
3. He used .... much more.
4. He promised me never .... so much again.
5. We don't know where ....
6. I'd rather .... late than early.
7. He'd better .... less.
8. Can you make him .... less?
9. Has he always .... so much?
10. He .... very little when he was younger.
11. He keeps .... the whole day long.
12. He can't go without .... at least ten times a day!

IV. *Fill in with* **do, doing, make,** *or* **making.**

1. Mother is .... the dishes.
2. He's going to .... me a favor.
3. I hope you won't .... any mistakes.
4. Mr. Brown is .... a speech.
5. He will .... a good impression on his audience.
6. You must .... an effort and work harder.
7. I'm .... some work for my father right now.
8. I .... all the decisions.
9. Don't .... a habit of smoking.
10. She's .... her homework.
11. .... you help your mother?
12. Is Jim .... a bookcase?

In this unit we are going to read and talk about people who love adventure and enjoy taking chances.

We are going to study and practice making sentences like:
Why is Sid so good at **skiing?**
He's a good **skier** because he practices skiing every day.

He was born **in** 1803.	He was born **in** Barcelona.
He was born **in** Spain.	He was born **on** July 1st.
He was born **in** the spring.	He was born **at** a hospital.

We are also going to use these vocabulary words:

absolutely	gymnastics	retire
adventurous	huge	risk
box	jog	stupid
boxer	jogger	seasons
centuries	mind *(v.)*	skin dive
century	nerve	skin diver
climber	pastime	training
corner	practice	win
drag racing	problem	wrestling
fans	professional	wrestler
gymnast	refuse	

WARM-UP

—Who do you think will win?
—Well, the Brazilian had the fastest time in training.
—But can he stay on the track?
—That's a good question.
—I think he takes too many chances.
—He enjoys taking chances.

SMALL TALK

—Do you often **play football?**
—Oh, yes. I really enjoy **playing football.** (or)
—No, I don't enjoy **playing football.**

1.   2.   3.   4.

How About You?
1. Do you often go to the races?
2. Do you often play golf?
3. Do you often go mountain-climbing?
4. Do you often read adventure stories?
5. Do you often go sailing?

—What do you do all day?
—**Sleep.**
—You mean you spend your time **sleeping?**
—I most certainly do.

1. **practice baseball**   2. **jog**   3. **box**

4. **mountain-climb**   5. **skin dive**   6. **sail**

READ AND UNDERSTAND

Drag Racing

You have probably seen sports-car racing on TV or at the movies. But have you ever seen a drag race? Drag racing started in the United States in 1953.

The first drag tracks were built by people who were worried about teen-agers who were racing their cars in public streets. A track is an absolutely straight course about 1200 feet long. The track has to be straight because the cars go so fast that they cannot possibly take a corner. Each race lasts only about seven seconds!

The cars used in drag racing don't have much in common with other racing cars. In the front is something that looks like a bicycle wheel. Huge, fat tires are at the back. A powerful engine is usually in front of the driver. During a race there is sometimes so much smoke from the engines and the burning rubber from the tires that it's hard to see the cars. The fans don't mind. They say the best races are those where the cars go so fast you can't see them at all!

Drag racing has changed from a teen-age pastime to big business. There are professional races now. A good drag racer can earn as much as $65,000 a year.

1. How long ago was drag racing started?
2. Why doesn't a drag track have any corners?
3. Why is it sometimes impossible to see the racers?
4. About how long does a race last?
5. Why are some drivers willing to risk their lives drag racing?

STUDY AND PRACTICE

—Why is Sid so good at **skiing?**
—He's a good **skier** because he practices **skiing** every day.

1. **skin diving**   2. **wrestling**   3. **climbing**
   skin diver   **wrestler**   **climber**

4. **boxing**   5. **jogging**   6. **gymnastics**
   boxer   **jogger**   **gymnast**

—Why does Peter hate **swimming?**
—Maybe it's because he's bad at **swimming.**

1.   2.

3.   4.

Fran wants to go to the races, but she has a problem. She has no way to get there, nothing to wear, and no money for the tickets! She decides to call her friend Pat.

—Hi, Pat. Would you like to go to the races today?

—Great! Can you lend me your blue jacket?

—Can you drive your car?

—Can you pick me up?

—Can you take me home?

—Can you pick up the tickets?

—Can you pay for them, too?

—Oh. Then we can't go.

—Okay, I don't mind going.

—Yes, I don't mind lending it to you.

—Yes, I don't mind driving.

—Yes, I don't mind picking you up.

—Yes, I don't mind taking you home.

—Yes, I don't mind picking up the tickets.

—No. I don't have any money.

—That's okay with me. I don't mind.

In, On, and At

Use **in** *with years.*

Henry Ford was born in 1863.
He founded his company in 1903.

Use **in** *with centuries.*

I was born in the 20th century.
Ford was born in the 19th cent▸

Use **in** *with months and seasons.*

I'm going to Spain in May.
The weather is warm in spring.

Use **in** *with cities and countries.*

Pete's in Chicago this week.
Hockey is popular in Canada.

Use **on** *with days and dates.*

He was born on January 1st, 1930.
He was born on the first of January.
I'm playing tennis on Friday.
We're leaving on the fifteenth.

Use **at** *with times and places.*

Meet me at eight o'clock.
Meet me at the library.
I get up at six every day.
I'm at the drugstore.

Now practice making sentences with these words. Be careful!

He was born	in on at	the evening. six o'clock. a Monday. Baker Hospital. Argentina. June 6th. the 18th century. home. the winter. 1945. Boston. a Saturday.

Complete these sentences with **in, on,** *or* **at.**
1. There's no school .... Saturdays.
2. He was born .... a Monday .... June.
3. Fred is .... the library .... Boston.
4. .... spring, I play tennis .... Tuesdays.
5. Meet me .... six o'clock .... the airport .... Chicago.

DIALOGUE

Have you heard about Ralph?

Yes, isn't he adventurous?
Yes, isn't he stupid?

What do you mean?
Do you think so?

He takes too many chances.
Yes, he enjoys risking his life.

He spends all his time
    practicing.
He's never at home.

You have to practice every
    day.
I know. I'm sure his family
    minds.

Do you really think that it's
    worth it?
But it's worth it, isn't it?

No, I don't think so.
I'm sure it is.

Does he earn a lot of money?

Yes, he's made a fortune.
No, but he enjoys being
    famous.

When do you think he'll
    retire?
Think he'll ever give it up?

Not before he kills himself.
I doubt it.

Would you like his job?

I wouldn't mind the money.
Not on your life. I haven't
    the nerve for it.

Neither would I.
Neither have I.

MIXED BAG

Look at all the pictures. Talk about the story with a friend. Then write down the story in your own words. These questions will help you.

1. What does Will ask Ruth one day?
2. What does she reply?
3. Why doesn't Ruth want to marry Will?
4. What does Will do then?
5. Where do Will and Ruth get married?
6. What sort of life do they have then?
7. What happens one day in town?
8. What happens to the stage coach?
9. What do the townspeople say?
10. What do they say to Will?
11. What does Ruth think about it all?
12. Does Will get out his guns, or does he refuse to help?
13. What happens next?
14. What does Will do when he gets home?

In this unit we are going to read and talk about inventors and the things they invent.

We are going to study and practice making sentences like:

I live **at** 24 Bank Street.　　John lives **with** his mother.
My house is **by** the lake.　　Mary is afraid **of** dogs.
This book is **for** Tom.　　Boston is **on** the Charles River.
He's sitting **in** the car.

We are also going to use these vocabulary words:

aid	device	rubbing
annual	designed	sewing machine
anti-snoring	examples	springs *(n.)*
automatically	instamatic	sticks
ball-point pen	inventors	straps
burglar	light bulb	tractor
classical	printing press	vase
deeply	peels	wheel

WARM-UP

—What do you think of my new invention?
—Unbelievable. What can it do?
—Absolutely anything.
—Ask it to go away, then.

SMALL TALK

—What's the most important invention ever made?
—The **wheel.** Don't you agree?
—I'm not so sure.
—What do you think, then?
—The **printing press.**

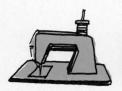

1. **light bulb   telephone**

2. **sewing machine   radio**

3. **airplane   car**

4. **credit card   TV**

5. **camera   tape recorder**

6. **tractor   clock**

READ AND UNDERSTAND

Inventors and Inventions

There is an annual Inventors' Fair in New York City every year. Inventors show their inventions to businessmen in hopes that they might buy them. Every inventor hopes to make a fortune from his ideas. It is a classical American dream—a poor man invents something and becomes the richest man in the world. The dream seldom comes true, however. Here are some of the inventions shown at a recent fair.

An anti-snoring device to help wives whose husbands snore in their sleep. It is a piece of plastic which the sleeper has to keep in his mouth all night!

An elegant clock designed by a Swiss dentist. Instead of working with weights or springs, it works with water.

Night-glasses for reading in bed. The glasses have little lamps fitted to them.

A special umbrella connected to a hat with chin straps. It is designed for people whose arms are full of packages.

Of course, not all inventions are strange or silly. Many are useful, and *do* make money for the inventors. Don't you wish you were the person who invented the instamatic camera, the clock-radio, color television, electric toothbrushes, or ball-point pens?

1. What is the Inventors' Fair?
2. Why do people dream of becoming successful inventors?
3. Do you think any of the inventions mentioned are good? Why or why not?
4. Do you have an invention of your own that you think could make you a fortune?

STUDY AND PRACTICE

An unhappy young man is looking at a photo of a beautiful girl. He is telling his friend that there is another man in the girl's life.

—Did the other man see her first?

—Did he say hello first?

—Did he take her out that night?

—Did he take her dancing?

—Did he buy her dinner?

—Did he kiss her good-night?

—Did he send her flowers?

—Did he write her love letters?

—Did he buy her jewelry?

—Did he love her deeply?

—Did he ask her to marry him?

—Well, did she marry you?

—No, he didn't. I saw her first.

—No, he didn't. I said hello first.

—No, he didn't. I took her out.

—No, he didn't. I took her dancing.

—No, he didn't. I bought her dinner.

—No, he didn't. I kissed her.

—No, he didn't. I sent her flowers.

—No, he didn't. I wrote her love letters.

—No, he didn't. I bought her jewelry.

—No, he didn't. I loved her deeply.

—No, he didn't. I asked her to marry me.

—No, she didn't. She married *him*.

At, By, and **For**

at

> —Where do you live?
> —I live at 24 Bank Street.

1. Where is John staying?   a hotel
2. Where did you see him?   a party
3. Where is your father?   work
4. When will she arrive?   the end of the week

by

> —Where's he sitting?
> —He's sitting by the window.

1. Where's your house?   the river
2. How did you travel?   train
3. How did you send the letter?   air mail
4. How did you break the vase?   accident

for

> —Why did you get that book?
> —I got it for Tom.

1. When did you get that watch?   my birthday
2. Why did you buy this ham?   lunch
3. What did he ask you for?   directions
4. Why was he arrested?   stealing
5. How long have you been away?   a long time

in

—Where's he sitting? —He's sitting in the car.

1. Where's London?

2. Where did you read about it?

3. When did you meet him?

4. When are they coming?

of

—What's Mary afraid of? —She's afraid of dogs.

1. What's your dress made of?

2. What's she tired of?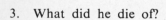

3. What did he die of?

4. What's your boat made of?

on

1. Who can she count on?

2. Where did you hear it?

3. Where's Boston?

4. When are you leaving?

5. What's he working on?

with

—Who does Jim live with? —He lives with his mother.

1. Who's Jill in love with?

2. How did she make her dress?

3. Who are you staying with?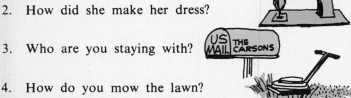

4. How do you mow the lawn?

DIALOGUE

Yes, may I help you?

I need a wedding present.
I need supplies for my office.

Right this way.
That department is over here.

What's the latest kitchen aid?
What will save me time?

This is the latest invention.
This is a fantastic typewriter.

What makes it different?
What does it do?

It peels and cuts up tomatoes.
It's electric, and corrects mistakes automatically.

That doesn't seem very useful.
I don't make mistakes.

How about this new machine?
Can you guess what this tape recorder does?

Records your voice, I suppose.
What does it do?

It turns the stove on and off.
Yes, but it starts automatically at the sound of your voice.

What's this thing?
Is this a clock?

A dishwasher and glass polisher.
No, it's a burglar alarm.

Sorry, I don't want any of these things.
I'll take everything.

Is there anything else?

How about an automatic

husband?
wife?
secretary?

Next year, I promise you!

MIXED BAG

Here are some inventions that man has made. Look at each of the examples below carefully. Then choose which invention you think each person is talking about.

1. I'm tired of carrying these rocks. I wish somebody would invent . . .

2. I'm tired of rubbing sticks together. I wish . . .

3. I'm tired of these long trips.

4. I'm tired of reading in this bad light.

5. I'm tired of shouting.

6. I'm tired of freezing at night.

In this unit we are going to read and talk about people's personalties and how they behave.

We are going to study and practice making sentences like:

Jim is very **selfish,** isn't he?
Oh, no! He's very **unselfish.**

We are also going to use these vocabulary words:

bellboy	selfish
definitions	smart
depend	stingy
generous	talented
honest	tease
humorous	trustworthy
ignorant	unselfish
questionnaire	well-educated
sense of humor	witty

WARM-UP

—I have a new boyfriend.
—What's he like?
—He's very talented and intelligent.
—What else?
—He's well-educated and handsome.
—What does he do?
—Oh, nothing. He's out of work right now.
—Why?
—He's the laziest man I've ever met.

SMALL TALK

Study the words and definitions below carefully. Then use the words in the dialogue below the box.

a generous man

a stingy man

ambitious	works very hard to become successful	unambitious
energetic	full of energy; hard-working	lazy
generous	willing to share; big-hearted	stingy
humorous	funny; witty; a person who can even laugh at himself has a good sense of humor	dull; humorless
honest	always truthful, trustworthy	dishonest
intelligent	clever; smart; bright	stupid
patient	willing to wait or try to do something for a long time without getting upset or giving up	impatient
unselfish	generous, never thinking of himself first	selfish
well-educated	one who has learned a lot at school and not wasted his time	ignorant

—John's very **handsome,** isn't he?
—Oh, no! He's very **ugly!**

READ AND UNDERSTAND

My Friend Charles

Whenever I have a party, Charles is always the first person I invite. He is such fun. I know that he will be able to make my other guests laugh. He doesn't get upset if somebody tries to tease or make fun of him, either. Charles can also be very serious and can discuss almost anything you can think of. If it gets late before the party ends, I can always depend on Charles to drive some of the guests home. He never says no, even if he is very tired and would rather go straight home to bed.

Charles is the manager of the motel on Lawndale Road. It's hard to believe that he was just a bellboy there only five years ago.

1. Do you think Charles has a sense of humor? Why or why not?
2. Do you think Charles is unselfish? Why or why not?
3. Do you think Charles is an ignorant person? Why or why not?
4. Do you think Charles is ambitious? Why or why not?

Len Cobbins

Len Cobbins was a farmer in the village where I spent my childhood. He was not a very good farmer, and never had any money. That was because he never worked very hard. He said he didn't care about building his small farm into anything important. I don't think Len could even read or write.

One night, somebody stole a lot of money from the post office. My father said, "I'll bet it was old Len Cobbins. Poor old Len — he's sure to be caught." My father was right. Two days after the robbery, Len showed up in the village with a brand-new car! He just couldn't wait to spend the money. When the police asked him where he got the car, he said he found it. Poor old Len wasn't the brightest man I ever knew.

Underline the words you think describe Len Cobbins. Then tell why you chose each word.

1. energetic
2. lazy
3. ambitious
4. well-educated
5. ignorant
6. generous
7. dishonest
8. patient
9. impatient
10. intelligent
11. stupid
12. hard-working

DIALOGUE

Wow! Isn't this party terrific?

> No, there are too many guests.
> No, its too hot and noisy.

But haven't you met any interesting people?

> Not really. They all look unintelligent and boring.
> All the girls are ugly and silly.

> Sally isn't. She's very intelligent.
> Frank is a very ambitious architect.

> Maybe so. But he has no sense of humor.
> She thinks she's so clever — and she *is* ugly.

Have you talked with Randy?

Why? What does *he* do?

> He's a very energetic teacher.
> He's an honest banker.
> He's a well-educated critic.

> Oh, they're all dishonest.
> Oh, they're all ignorant.
> Oh, they're all lazy.

> Pat has a great sense of humor.
> Stan is nice. He's so unselfish.
> Judy is a talented singer.

> I can't stand her jokes.
> She sings much too loudly.
> He's too good to be true.

Why don't you leave if you're having such an awful time?

Unfortunately, I live here.
This is *my* party.

MIXED BAG

Fill in the questionnaire below. Be honest about yourself!

	5 Immensely	3 About average	2 A little	0 Not at all
1. Are you ambitious?				
2. Are you generous?				
3. Are you honest?				
4. Are you patient?				
5. Are you intelligent?				
6. Are you well-educated?				
7. Are you hard-working?				
8. Do you have a good sense of humor?				
9. Are you trustworthy?				
10. Are you unselfish?				

Your Score: 45-50 Are you sure you're *that* good?
                  40-45 Aren't you just a little dishonest?
                  25-40 You're like most people.
                  15-25 Are you giving yourself enough credit?
                    5-15 You need help!

TEST YOURSELF

I.
1. Did you see the car first?   No, my wife .... it first.
2. Did you phone the dealer?   No, my wife .... him.
3. Did you send for the catalogue? No, my wife .... for it.
4. Did you meet the salesman?   No, my wife .... him.
5. Did your wife buy the car?   No, she .... a motorcycle instead!

II. *Fill in with* **in, on,** *or* **at.**
1. He was born .... 7:53 .... December 25th.
2. .... winter, I usually try to take a vacation.
3. I first met him .... 1942.
4. We are living .... the twentieth century.
5. The garden looks beautiful .... the evening.
6. I'll see you .... Monday.
7. Meet me .... the airport .... Madrid .... January 5th.

II. *Fill in with* **practice, practices, practicing, practiced,** *or* **to practice.**
1. I enjoy golf. I .... almost every day.
2. He spends all his time .... golf.
3. She doesn't mind if her husband .... golf all day.
4. If you want to be a good golfer, you have .... often.
5. I .... every day when I used to play golf.

V. *Fill in with* **at, by, of, on,** *or* **for.**
1. He drove .... full speed.
2. I broke the glass .... accident.
3. He's very proud .... his son.
4. They live .... $50 a month.
5. What's your sweater made ....?
6. He was arrested .... stealing.

V.

(13) 1. What's she good at? ....

2. The is an important invention. ....

3. Their house is on the ....

4. She's proud of her ....

5. The is certainly useful. ....

6. The is part of the fashion world. ....

VI.

(14) 1. Ambitious is the opposite of ....
2. Lazy is the opposite of ....
3. Generous is the opposite of ....
4. Honest is the opposite of ....
5. Patient is the opposite of ....
6. Selfish is the opposite of ....

VII.

Complete this dialogue. There is more than one "right" answer for each blank.

1. .... —Kitchen goods are over there
2. .... —This is the latest thing.
3. .... —It peels and cuts potatoes.
4. .... —No, it's quite inexpensive.
5. .... —Only $95.
6. .... —No, we accept only cash.

WORD LIST

The following is a list of words and expressions introduced in this book. The numbers shown refer to the pages where the words first appear.

absolutely 121
acceptable 32
acting 2
actor 26
actress 24
ad 22
advantage 61
adventurous 125
advertising 52
afford 61
agent 43
agree 108
ahead 55
aid 136
allow 36
amazed 6
ambitious 110
amount 61
amused 32
announced 43
announcer 109
annual 131
anti-snoring 131
anxiously 12
appearing 21
architects 86
aspirin 53
astronaut 109
attacked 12
audience 22
autographs 22
automatically 136

back seat driver 2

ball-point pen 131
bargain 41
bathing suit 42
beer 22
behave 16
behavior 32
bellboy 141
borrowed 110
brakes 8
brand-new 80
breathe 18
brewery 52
brightly 12
brillant 24
broadcast 12
bureau 53
burglar 136
business 61

calmly 15
campaign 52
canvas 44
careful 18
car dealer's 3
careless 15
catalogue 61
cemetery 82
center 86
centuries 124
century 124
ceremony 90
certain 61
change *(money)* 95
chance 37

charity 22
check 22
checked *(adj.)* 43
childhood 115
citizens 6
classical 131
climate 27
club 22
clues 105
coaches 90
coincidence 36
collar 42
collection 43
combinations 43
commission 61
common 110
companies 61
compare 55
conductor 26
confident 80
confused 52
conventional 96
considered 32
contain 66
continued 12
controls (n) 100
corner 121
correct 14
cotton 44
creature 11
credit 61
creeping 100
critics 28
cuffs 43
customers 61
customs 19

damaged 71
daring 42
decisions 113
deeply 132
definitely 28
definitions 140
dentist 109
department store
depend 141
designed 131
desk 64
detail 66
detergent 51
device 131
differ 32
direct *(adj.)* 95
directions 29
directory 69
disadvantages 61
disappeared 106
disconnected 100
diseases 115
disturb 85
down payment 61
drag racing 121
dressing room 22
drugstore 45
during 8

easy 69
economical 3
electric 60
electrician 109
elegant 14
emergency 68
employment 115
energetic 110
engine 71
engineer 109
entertainer 24
entertainment 25

enthusiastic 22
exactly 29
examples 137
excellent 24
expected 89
explosion 12
extra 112

failing 113
familiar 29
fans 121
fantastic 22
farthest 9
fascinating 24
fashionable 42
fast 3
fattening 51
fault 31
favor 113
fear *(n)* 90
female 110
fingerprints 105
fire department 68
five-pound notes 100
flash 12
flat *(tire)* 85
fond 3
fooled 18
fortune 108
forward 102
founded 6
freezing 27
frequently 17
froze 90

gallon 54
gang 98
gasoline 9
gasped 29
generous 140
germ 12

ghosts 82
gossiping 45
grandparents 17
grocery store 51
gum 54
gymnastics 122

habit 113
hair spray 54
hammer 53
hang 43
hardware store 53
harmless 12
heard 14
hers 34
high-powered 51
hire 110
hitchhiking 78
holes 19
honest 140
horn 73
household goods 61
huge 121
human 115
humorous 140

idol 21
ignorant 140
ignore 52
immensely 33
impatient 15
impolite 32
impression 110
in person 21
insisted 29
instamatic 131
invaders 12
invention 14
inventors 131
investing 108
item 61

jealous 27
jog 120
judges 113

knife 32

lap 32
lawyer 109
least 51
leather 6
lend 108
lent 110
light bulb 130
lighter *(adj.)* 6
lipstick 51
live *(adj.)* 21
loaf *(n.)* 54
lobster 53
locomotive 90
loose 42

magnificent 14
mail-order 61
main 61
manage 36
management 115
manners 32
marched 22
margarine 50
marvelous 14
matches 94
materials 43
matter 33
maximum 9
mechanic 109
mechanical 6
medical 70
medicine 53
mention 36
merchandise 59
might 32

mileage 9
mind *(v.)* 123
mine 34
mines 6
mix-up 52
monsoon 110
motor 6
musician 22
must 14
mysterious 12

neither 12
nerve 125
nervous 8
newsstand 51
nobleman 32
nonsense 82
normal 12
notice *(v.)* 69
nowadays 82
now and then 17
nylon 44

object *(n.)* 12
obviously 100
occur 69
once 55
operated 70
operator 68
opposite 16
orchestra 26
ours 22
outfit 48
out of order 100
oversleep 85

pack *(n.)* 54
pale 27
panicked 90
pantsuit 42
pardon 93

parlor 96
pastime 121
patterned 42
payments 60
peas 32
pedestrian 2
peels 136
percent 60
perfect 28
performance 21
performer 22
perfume 51
phrases 70
planet 12
plastic 44
poetry 45
point *(n.)* 55
pointing 18
poisonous 69
polite 15
politicians 113
polka-dot 42
poll 11
possibly 31
powerful 4
prefers 50
price 9
printed 63
printing press 130
prison 70
producing 6
product 52
professional 121
promise 85
propeller 110
protected 71
proud 14
prove 110
public 52
purse 29

questionnaire 14
quit 64

ray *(gun)* 18
real 22
rear-view mirror 84
reasons 61
reassure 114
refunded 59
refuse 126
repaired 86
replace 80
rescue 110
resist 22
respectable 42
rest rooms 99
retire 125
reviews 28
rewarded 71
rice 51
risk 121
roadblock 71
robot 14
rocky 79
roof 68
route 110
rubber 44
rubbing 137

safe 3
salesman 3
sample 55
sandstorm 110
saucers 11
scissors 54
scream 12
script 114
seafood 53
seasick 27
seasons 124
seat covers 84

seems 91
selfish 140
sense of humor 140
served 32
set 84
sewing machine 130
shining 12
ships 6
shocked 27
shopper 61
short cut 8
shrimp 53
silk 44
simply 22
sinking 69
situation 69
size 66
skin dive 120
sleeveless 42
sleeves 43
soap 51
social 32
soldiers 12
sorted 62
sounds *(n.)* 19; *(v.)* 21
special 47
speech 26
spray 54
springs *(n.)* 131
squad car 68
stage 21
stamp 99
star 29
station wagon 3
steam 90
stereo 60
sticks 137
stingy 140
stood 19
stove 60
stranger 29

straps 131
striking *(adj.)* 48
striped 42
stupid 125
style 43
successful 6
such 14
suitable 104
suits *(v.)* 41
sum 6
superb 14
suppose 3

tank 9
tease 141
teen-age 22
terrific 45
theirs 34
thick 79
tight 42
tools 53
toothpaste 54
total 61
track 89
tractor 130
training 119
troubles 57
trousers 42
trustworthy 140
tube 54
twice 55

unbelievable 80
uncomfortable 32
unfortunately 110
university 110
unloaded 100
unselfish 140
unusual 110
useless 12

Answers to *Test Yourself Sections*

Pp. 38-39

I.   1. gas *or* gasoline 2. vehicles 3. factory 4. expensive 5. harmless 6. polite 7. weapons 8. station 9. dry 10. enthusiastic 11. dressing room 12. terrible 13. impolite 14. uncomfortable 15. You're welcome. 16. Pleased to meet you. 17. Pardon?

II.   1. many 2. more 3. less *or* more

III.   1. best 2. most economical 3. safest 4. marvelous, superb, *or* magnificent 5. superbly, magnificently, *or* marvelously 6. angry 7. angry

IV.   1. What a 2. What 3. What

V.   1. yourselves 2. yourself 3. yours 4. you

VI.   1. You're driving too fast.; You're speeding. 2. The one that said Do Not Enter; No Left Turn; No Right Turn. 3. But it's a one-way street.; But the sign said Do Not Enter.; But the sign said No Left Turn; No Right Turn. 4. I wish you'd slow down.; Don't drive so fast. 5. Are we in a hurry?; Are you taking the short cut? 6. Stop the car.

Pp. 74-76

I.   clothing store, campaign, fashions, collection, daring, agent, hair, shorter, bald, easy, detergent.

II.   1. a pound of butter 2. a pair of scissors 3. a gallon of paint 4. a pack of cigarettes 5. a loaf of bread 6. a box of nails 7. a tube of lipstick 8. a can of hair spray 9. a pack of gum

III.   1. wore 2. drove 3. bought

IV.   1. bought 2. buy 3. bought 4. buy 5. buys

V.   1. deliver 2. delivered 3. delivers 4. delivered

VI.   1. where 2. who 3. what 4. where 5. what 6. who

Pp. 116-117

I. 1. tremendous 2. panicked 3. knocked 4. wallet
5. coaches 6. bridge 7. obviously 8. escaped
9. finger-prints 10. medical school 11. reward

II. 1. When is the next train to Washington?; When does the next train to Washington leave? 2. What time does it arrive? 3. How much is the fare?; How much is the ticket? 4. Is that round-trip, or one-way? 5. Is it on time?; Will it arrive on time?

III. 1. eats 2. to eat 3. to eat 4. to eat 5. to eat 6. eat
7. eat 8. eat 9. eaten 10. ate 11. eating 12. eating

IV. 1. doing 2. do 3. make 4. making 5. make 6. make
7. doing 8. make 9. make 10. doing 11. Do 12. making

Pp. 145-146

I. 1. saw 2. phoned 3. sent 4. met 5. bought

II. 1. at, on 2. In 3. in 4. in 5. in 6. on 7. at, in, on

III. 1. practice 2. practicing 3. practices 4. to practice
5. practiced

IV. 1. at 2. by 3. of 4. on 5. of 6. for

V. 1. skin diving 2. light bulb 3. coast 4. ring 5. wheel
6. sewing machine

VI. 1. unambitious 2. energetic 3. stingy 4. dishonest
5. impatient 6. unselfish

VII. 1. I need something for the kitchen.; Where are the kitchen goods? 2. What's the latest kitchen aid?; What's the latest thing? 3. What does it do?; What makes it different? 4. I suppose it's very expensive.; Is it expensive? 5. *How* inexpensive?; How much exactly? 6. Can I charge it?; Can I pay for it on time?; Can I write you a check?